T0323693

Cambridge Elements ≡

Elements in Feminism and Contemporary Critical Theory
edited by
Jennifer Cooke
Loughborough University
Amber Jamilla Musser
CUNY Graduate Center
Juno Jill Richards
Yale University

THIS WILL NOT BE GENERATIVE

Dixa Ramírez-D'Oleo
Brown University

CAMBRIDGE
UNIVERSITY PRESS

CAMBRIDGE
UNIVERSITY PRESS

Shaftesbury Road, Cambridge CB2 8EA, United Kingdom

One Liberty Plaza, 20th Floor, New York, NY 10006, USA

477 Williamstown Road, Port Melbourne, VIC 3207, Australia

314–321, 3rd Floor, Plot 3, Splendor Forum, Jasola District Centre,
New Delhi – 110025, India

103 Penang Road, #05–06/07, Visioncrest Commercial, Singapore 238467

Cambridge University Press is part of Cambridge University Press & Assessment,
a department of the University of Cambridge.

We share the University's mission to contribute to society through the pursuit of
education, learning and research at the highest international levels of excellence.

www.cambridge.org
Information on this title: www.cambridge.org/9781009320320

DOI: 10.1017/9781009320337

First published 2023

A catalogue record for this publication is available from the British Library.

ISBN 978-1-009-32032-0 Paperback
ISSN 2754-303X (online)
ISSN 2754-3021 (print)

Cambridge University Press & Assessment has no responsibility for the persistence
or accuracy of URLs for external or third-party internet websites referred to in this
publication and does not guarantee that any content on such websites is, or will
remain, accurate or appropriate.

This Will Not Be Generative

Elements in Feminism and Contemporary Critical Theory

DOI: 10.1017/9781009320337
First published online: March 2023

Dixa Ramírez-D'Oleo
Brown University

Author for correspondence: Dixa Ramírez-D'Oleo, dixa_ramirez@brown.edu

Abstract: *This Will Not Be Generative* attends to the semiotics of ecological writings via Caribbean literary studies and black critical theory. Closely reading texts by Donna Haraway, Monique Allewaert, and Lisa Wells, it exposes how the language of tentacles and tendrils, an assumptive "we," and redemptive sympathy or "care" disguises extraction from black people and blackness. This often speculative rhetoric, abetted by fantasies of white communion with Indigenous groups, contrasts with the horror semiotics of the films *Get Out* (2017) and *Midsommar* (2019), which unmask the antagonistic relationship between white survival "at the end of the world" and blackness as compost.

Keywords: black critical theory, Anthropocene, literary studies, speculative fabulation, eco-criticism/ecological writings

ISBNs: 9781009320320 (PB), 9781009320337 (OC)
ISSNs: 2754-303X (online), 2754-3021 (print)

Contents

1 Exergue

At my godmother Olga's, in the late 1980s, there was fresh limeade and clinking ice served in the shade of a trumpet tree.[1] At my grandmother Deidamia's nearby, I shelled peas on weekend and summer mornings while Grandma swung a chicken by its neck till dead, to be de-feathered and marinated in sour orange and cilantro. Both women handled citrus and poultry with bejeweled and manicured fingers. Their shared high femininity offset the class and race differences of my godmother's white elite status and my grandmother's educated black and rural background. Their gardens, one elevated on a second-floor terrace and the other on the ground itself, overflowed with bougainvillea, hibiscus, rose bushes, cordyline, ferns, and all kinds of striped crotons. Lime, mango, and plantain trees provided beauty and nourishment. My grandmother, like many women and men of her generation, could look at almost any plant and list its curative uses. During her visits to our new home in the South Bronx in the early 1990s, she would interrupt her stride, point to something green growing from the cracked sidewalk, and tell me what medicinal Caribbean plant it conjured. Her voice always had a tinge of reverence and what I can only describe as love – love for this replica plant that reminded her of something back home, love for the plant back home, and love of this knowledge. These replica plants then helped soothe a homesickness so profound that few memories remain of my first years in the United States. Like the swelling sea of auto shops that surrounded them, Deidamia's and Olga's Santo Domingo gardens sprouted in the crevices between the tropical Caribbean wilderness, what I have written about elsewhere as *el monte*, and the growing capital city (Ramírez-D'Oleo 2019, 2021a, 2021b, and 2022). The wilderness always threatened to reclaim its territory; we, the new arrivants, were reminded that we were interlopers by the frequent appearance of "critters" like tarantulas, frogs, and giant red centipedes. Olga's garden has since been replaced by a dermatology clinic and its parking lot, and a cramped stack of small apartments sits atop the memory of my grandmother's garden.

I would caution against misreading this exergue as a sedimentation of my "identity," "culture," and "otherness," or misreading it as a symptom of O, who, as described by Rey Chow, is a figure from the "third world" in the North American academy who brandishes her identity in exchange for popularity, and as unmoored from intellectual expertise (Chow 1998: 26–30).

---

[1] The *grayumbo* tree or the *Cecropia schreberiana*.

2 Introduction

> "My multispecies storytelling is about recu-
> peration in complex histories that are full of
> dying as living, as full of endings, even
> genocides, as beginnings."
> Donna Haraway, *Staying with the Trouble*[2]

> " . . . turbulent but generative . . . "
> Donna Haraway, *Staying with the Trouble*[3]

Organized by my readerly journey from seduction to recoil, *This Will Not Be Generative* focuses on various works by Donna Haraway to demonstrate how the ludic language of tendrils and tentacles costumes a violent relationship to "the black(ened) position."[4] I also analyze Monique Allewaert's study of anglophone colonial texts, *Ariel's Ecology: Plantations, Personhood, and Colonialism in the American Tropics* (2013), and Lisa Wells's *New York Times* nonfiction bestseller, *Believers: Making Life at the End of the World* (2021). I read these texts closely and with methods inspired by Caribbean literary studies, black critical theory, and the theoretical innovations of various procedures of negative criticism and deconstruction.[5] The Caribbean studies that influence my writing are centered on the long history of refusals of European temporalities on the island that now encompasses the Dominican Republic and Haiti.[6] The black critical theory to which I refer is similarly specific, loosely defined by its focus on how anti-blackness shapes the world. I contend that Haraway's, Allewaert's, and Wells's "urgent" ecological discourses attempt to disguise within them a grammar in which whiteness can survive as white *indigène* (a kind of North American *mestizaje*) through the expectation of non-African Indigenous tutelage. In these discourses, blackness, which is never also Indigenous in these writings, continues performing the function it has had in Western epistemes as that which must be

---

[2] Haraway 2016b: 10.   [3] Haraway 2016b: 145.

[4] I define the black or black(ened) position after Jared Sexton paraphrasing Frank B. Wilderson III to include "those marked by racial blackness, including most especially African-derived people" (Sexton 2016). Blackness as discussed here is not an identity; rather, it is a structural position that signals usability for others' desires (material, libidinal, emotional, and beyond). People of African descent are marked by blackness due to the historical fact of *inherited* slave status that only befell people of African descent for centuries and structured the world in which we continue to live. There are circumstances in which people not of African descent experience the grammar of structural anti-blackness, but this is not the same as being fixed and marked by it perpetually.

[5] The discourse of generativity in ecological writings also has ramifications in fields and methods such as animal studies, new materialism, queer studies, geography, black ecology, science and technology studies, and biopolitics.

[6] I discuss some of these refusals in Ramírez-D'Oleo 2018 and 2022.

destroyed so that it can give life to other life-forms.[7] I contrast the disguising and obfuscating procedures of the speculative mode that these eco-critics embrace with the semiotics of horror in Jordan Peele's *Get Out* (2017) and Ari Aster's *Midsommar* (2019).

Writings, lectures, and symposia inspired by ecological collapse have become so pervasive in the US academy – not to mention in other institutions, such as the art world – that it would be impossible to scrutinize all the works that follow similar procedures. I have focused on limiting myself mostly to writings by Haraway, Allewaert, and Wells for several reasons. Within the established fields of the humanities and the social sciences that delve into ecological and biological matters, Haraway and Allewaert stand out as scholars who consider the histories of chattel slavery and colonialism in relation to climate change. My research focus on Caribbean literature, which delves into the histories of slavery and colonialism, helps explain my initial encounter with these two scholars. I additionally analyze Wells's writing because her position outside of academia renders her work a suitable case study of the pervasiveness and popularity of the rhetoric I discuss here. Haraway, as one of the most well-known scholars in the world – full stop – can be considered both an important progenitor and promoter of some of the rhetoric analyzed here, as well as exemplary of the kind of scholarship that seeks to straddle the sciences and nonsciences in the academy. Allewaert's book is also a case study of a literary studies attentive to the long history of vitalism as intertwined with more recent discussions of the environmental crisis.

While these works directly engage with the history of colonialism and, to a much lesser extent in the case of Haraway and Wells, slavery, they share the same blind spot of not considering how the position of white womanhood has historically abetted these same histories.[8] They contain assumptive or explicit critiques of white, phallogocentric Eurocentrism, but they also seek ways to reject complicity in the consequences of this white, phallogocentric Eurocentrism that we all continue to live. This phallogocentrism can take the form of "woman." In this sense, these texts are far from unique, but emerge, once again, as case studies to demonstrate a set of procedures that apply to many other works. I will focus on Haraway's work briefly to preview some of what I mean. Despite the moments in her work in which she explicitly criticizes white feminism, as she does in her famed "A Cyborg Manifesto: Science, Technology,

---

[7] The definition of the black(ened) position I follow here precludes it from "indigeneity." This is not to be confused with specific African cultures and people that can be considered Indigenous.

[8] There is a long history of critique of white femininity or womanhood, if not outright feminism, in black women's writing, including Harriet Jacobs's and Mary Prince's narratives, as well as Ida B. Wells's journalism. For recent, scholarly critiques, see Spivak 1999, Wexler 2000, Wilderson 2010, and Schuller 2018.

and Socialist-Feminism in the Late Twentieth Century," some of the grammar buttressing white feminism also structures Haraway's writings. For instance, several chapters in *Primate Visions*, which I analyze in Section 4, explain how white feminism improved primatology and how, in turn, these primatologists influenced Haraway's methods. Yet, *Primate Visions* does not also consider how all white women primatologists working in Africa remain *structurally* bound to repeat the same extractive systems of thought of the male hunter taxidermists whom she argues had preceded them. *Primate Vision*'s blind spot grows from an inability to imagine that the most liberal or even "radical" left ideological positions – including various strands of feminism – may remain bound to the structures of anti-blackness and white supremacy.[9]

Another common feature of the writings under discussion is their positivist or additive propensity. The "more" is just as likely to be rhetorical as physical or biological. In Haraway, "more" is also bound with pathos. "Caring," she writes, "means becoming subject to the unsettling obligation of curiosity, which requires knowing more at the end of the day than at the beginning" (Haraway 2008: 36). These writings encrust generativity with seemingly positive descriptors (e.g., "caring," "loving," "thick," and so on), disguising the destruction also taking place. Even in their rush to generate newfangled language that often distances a signifier from relevant historical and/or etymological context (replacements such as "seminal" to "generative" or "cthulhu" to "chthulu"), these writings all admit that some entity must be destroyed or absorbed for the hybrid (symbiotic) life-form to be realized. However, of the texts discussed here, only Wells's *Believers* dwells on this loss, which manifests as a cycle of guilt, shame, and desire for absolution. Another broad tendency in these writings is their being grounded in a secularized Protestant episteme, even as they also criticize the forms of colonialism undergirded by Protestantism and Christianity writ large. This tendency emerges in the underlying assumption that productivity (i.e., generativity) is an ethical, moral, biological, and semiotic *good*.

If humans are running out of time on the planet, any time and energy spent on matters not inspired by climate change are time and energy wasted. Does this rhetoric of urgency buttress arguments against scholarship that cannot account for how it has productive, if not always materialist, utility? Scholarship whose function is to analyze, critique, de-sediment, and question without necessarily being equally concerned with the work of *creating* –

---

[9] For an analysis of how the basis of radical politics in the Western world rely on racism and anti-blackness, see Rei Terada's "Hegel's Racism Is for Radicals" (Terada 2019).

beyond the critique itself – remains crucial in a world barreling into increasingly obvious fascisms. Susan Sontag's "Fascinating Fascisms" (1974) and Rey Chow's "The Fascist Longings in Our Midst" expose the grammars of subtle fascisms (Sontag 2002; Chow 1998). If one agrees with Sontag's and Chow's analyses, one may discover that the grammar and syntax of fascism has been lurking not only within the expected political right, but also within the most "radical" left corners of academia. I attribute a deep-seated suspicion of some language games both to my orientation toward symptomatic reading and to my upbringing in a (post-) authoritarian society.[10] For many Dominicans from the 1930s into the 1980s, survival often relied on public enunciations of a set of preapproved phrases, as well as the ability to discern hidden meanings behind florid language of love of nation and community. Fascism, as Sontag contends, is not a friend to critique. For instance, Sontag cites Joseph Goebbels's prohibition of art criticism due to its having "typically Jewish traits of character," such as "putting the head over the heart, the individual over the community, intellect over feeling" (Sontag 2002: 88). Goebbels ascribed critique (as analysis, at times negative) to "Jewish intellectualism," which had to be destroyed to allow for the rise of the "German spirit" (Sontag 2002: 88). In other words, rhetorics of pathos, community, vitality, and spirit have long been entwined with each other and against critique. I would argue that the US academy is amidst an anti-critical moment. This Element focuses on ecological writings to partly illuminate the tendencies of this moment.

Given the demand for, sometimes gimmicky, attempts at interdisciplinarity, on one end, and assurances that one's scholarship will provide healing and solace, on the other, writing critique-as-such is not a fashionable move for a scholar interested in the various manifestations of racial injustice, especially anti-blackness. The US academy's current (quite literal) investment in interdisciplinarity, while we also hear, ad nauseam, about the "crisis in the humanities," warrants further discussion beyond the confines of this Element. But it bears asking for whom is interdisciplinarity a gain and for whom is it a loss?

The rhetoric of urgency evident in ecological writings prompts the question of why grapple with the enduring and constitutive anti-blackness of the world considering "we already know" and "we all" will be extinct soon enough? As Patricia Stuelke asserts, the fallacy that "we already know" enough about the gross injustices of our world emerges in two field-shifting essays: Eve

---

[10] As recently as 2015, a Dominican rapper was indicted and punished for seeming to criticize the country's Founding Fathers (Ramírez-D'Oleo 2018: 111–113).

Sedgwick's "Paranoid Reading and Reparative Reading, Or, You Probably Think This Essay Is about You" (Sedgwick 2003) and Stephen Best's and Sharon Marcus's "Surface Reading: An Introduction" (Best and Marcus 2009).[11] Both essays critique the then-predominance of "paranoid" or symptomatic reading methods that suspiciously search for absences. From this perspective, paranoid and symptomatic readings are not only "arrogant" and "mean" but also "passé" and "futile."[12] In spite of the differences in what the essays call for – "reparative" reading methods in Sedgwick's and "surface" reading methods in Best's and Marcus's – it is worthwhile to note that they share the following element. The exorbitant policing, incarceration, and suffering of black people emerge in both essays as examples par excellence of: (1) just how awful things really are, and, therefore, (2) the need to do something else besides "exposing the [apparently obvious] ruses of power" (Stuelke 2021: 5).[13] In her critique of the turn to "repair" as a method in the humanities, Stuelke demonstrates that rebuttals of critique-as-such greatly overstate "the assumption that the mechanisms of state, imperialist, and racial capitalist violence are already known and understood" (Stuelke 2021: 9). Even more concerning is "how discourses of [an assumed] transparency themselves work to enforce ongoing forms of state violence and racial capitalist dispossession" (Stuelke 2021: 9). Writers moved by the similar signs of "care" or "repair" elevate specific kinds of pathos – benevolent, optimistic, or sympathetic – at the expense of methods that either avoid pathos or evoke affects such as "reticent," "uncooperative," or "withholding."[14] The demand that intellectual engagement conform to specific affective scripts through a gluttonous desire for generativity ironically silences a wide array of intellectual inquiry.

Many of these writings reinstate the violence of "good" intentions, sympathy, absolution, and redemption found in nineteenth-century abolitionist and sentimentalist narratives. The difference between the end of slavery in white-authored nineteenth-century abolitionist discourses and the struggle for emancipation

---

[11] Rey Chow also notes the "broad" influence of Sedgwick's essay against critique-as-such (Chow 2021: 12).

[12] The terms in quotation marks are from Stuelke's description of Sedgwick's take on paranoid critique (Stuelke 2021: 5). Haraway describes a specific moment in Gilles Deleuze and Félix Guattari's writing as "smart" and "mean," which is folded into her broader critique of their perspective on the wolf (Haraway 2008: 28).

[13] Sedgwick uses the example of "40 percent of young black men enmeshed in the penal system" (Sedgwick 2003: 140). Best and Marcus use the example of "the state's abandonment of its African American citizens" during Hurricane Katrina (Best and Marcus 2009: 2).

[14] For Haraway on "caring" and "care," see Haraway 2008: 82–85 and 332n8. For research on the violence of "care" and "love" in a slaveholding society, see Dayan 1998 and Johnson 2018.

evident in violent slave rebellions lies in the differences between an imaginary that assumes white survival and enduring control and one that destroys it. Similarly, many ecological writings presume that, even "at the end of the world" and after the "apocalypse," white survival and control – even in rhetorical symbiosis with local ecologies and as abetted by fantasies of communion with (non-African) Indigenous groups – will endure. Patricia Yaeger's concept of the "unthought known" is useful to consider here. After Christopher Bollas, Yaeger defines this concept as "the omnipresence of ideas that are known but not acknowledged" (Yaeger 2000: 101). Writing about US Southern women's literature, Yaeger also calls this an "everyday world of white unseeing" in which many literary works feature "white citizens' 'genuine shock' at encountering a world that they see every day – suggesting ... a deliberate sequestration of knowledge" (Yaeger 2000: 103). In her analysis, motifs of soil and burials make evident (or, more appropriately, submerge) the sublimation taking place. "In southern literature," she writes, "extraordinary numbers of [black] women, men, and children fall into the landscape and disappear. It is as if the foundation or basis for this world is made out of repudiated, throwaway bodies that mire the earth: a landscape built over and upon the melancholic detritus, the disposable bodies denied by white culture" (Yaeger 2000: 15). These bodies are "cast away without funerals, left unmourned" (Yaeger 2000: 18). In this Element, I read closely for "the unthought known" that sustains the grammar of these ecological writings. I show how a semiotics that seems to be liberatory and generative for an inclusive "we" remains reliant on a grammar of suffering and destruction for those in the black(ened) position. Finally, I argue that avoiding negative critique and semiotic destruction of texts seeming to operate with "good" (i.e., liberal or "radical") intentions relies on accepting the black(ened) position's perpetual destruction.

3 The Seduction

"If you see such a semiotic barnacle, scrape it off."
Donna Haraway, *Staying with the Trouble*[15]

I read *Staying with the Trouble* and other ecological writings or eco-criticism while conducting research for another book, *Blackness and the Photographic Negative*, in which I explore black Caribbean aesthetic and historical forms of anti-relation and refusals of European epistemic paradigms of capture.[16] In my focus on black Caribbean anti-relationality, at times reliant on entanglements

---

[15] Haraway 2016b: 169.   [16] Forthcoming from Duke University Press.

with local ecologies, I kept encountering what I consider forced or coerced relationality in various works of eco-criticism. Revisiting *Staying with the Trouble* a couple of years after my first perusal, and in juxtaposition with several of Haraway's earlier works and interviews, I deciphered the violent grammar that lurks beneath the seductive language of "critters" and "chthonic ones" (Haraway 2016b: 2). Haraway suggests that part of the eco-critic's responsibility is to use seduction to proselytize the message to nonbelievers. Referencing a text called "Gens, a Feminist Manifesto for the Study of Capitalism," Haraway complains that "the writing is perhaps too dry (although the summary bullet points help), and there are no juicy examples to make this Manifesto seduce the spoiled reader" (Haraway 2016b: 208n17). Spoiled, I first read *Staying with the Trouble* and its "juicy examples" with gusto.

The opening sentences may be enchanting for a reader (me) whose childhood nickname was *Cacata*, the Taino word for tarantula. "*Trouble*," announces Haraway,

> is an interesting word. It derives from a thirteenth-century French verb meaning "to stir up," "to make cloudy," "to disturb." We – all of us on Terra – live in disturbing times, mixed-up times, troubling and turbid times. The task is to become capable, with each other in all of our bumptious kinds, of response. Mixed-up times are overflowing with unnecessary killing of ongoingness but also with necessary resurgence. The task is to make kin in lines of inventive connection as a practice of learning to live and die well with each other in a thick present. Our task it to make trouble, to stir up potent response to devastating events, as well as to settle troubled waters and rebuild quiet places. (Haraway 2016b: 1)

Trouble, Terra, turbid, bumptious, resurgence, thick, stir up, rebuild: these are the words that excited me when I first encountered them – before the COVID-19 pandemic and the second Black Lives Matter Movement of 2020. Who knew that working toward a "resurgence" of the planet, Terra, could be described as "undulating with slippery eros and gravid chaos, tangled snakes and ongoing tentacular forces" (Haraway 2016b: 174)? "Critters – " Haraway writes, "human and not – become-with each other, compose and decompose each other, in every scale and register of time and stuff in sympoietic tangling, in ecological evolutionary developmental earthly worlding and unworlding" (Haraway 2016b: 97). For someone dubious of anthropocentric schemes, the term "critters" reads delightfully; to include so many kinds of life, including machines, within its purview seemed inventive. What other language games, words, movements, stories can be generated, bringing them to the discursive, speculative, and perhaps even material world? "It matters," writes Haraway, "what stories we tell to tell other stories with. It matters wherehow Ouroboros swallows its tale, again. That's how wording gets on with itself in dragon time. These are such simple and difficult koans; let us see what kind of get they spawn" (Haraway 2016b: 118). Through SF – Haraway's acronym for "science fiction, speculative fabulation, string figures, speculative feminism, science fact, so far" – the world is our oyster.[17] *Poiesis* may save us yet.

Haraway's writing is tenaciously ludic. Neologisms such as "wherewhenever" and "wherehow" exemplify the importance of "play" in her method. Some of her syntax reminds me of the Lewis Carroll poem "Jabberwocky" (1871), whose nonsense speech my prep school theater teacher forced us to memorize and recite in under thirty seconds. As an enunciation exercise, "Beware the JubJub bird, and shun / The frumious Bandersnatch" replaced our garbled repetitions of "unique New York unique New York." Fondly recalling mine and my friends' valorous attempts to recite the entire seven-stanza ballad poem without slurring our words, my South Bronx Dominican accent tripped syllabically over the fantastical image of the "frumious Bandersnatch" as much as the New York Jewish and WASPy accents of the other students. I can imagine words like "frumious" and "tulgey wood" in *Staying with the Trouble*, the imagined reader skipping over words like Alice in a world of enchanted nature. The playfulness of the inadvertently multiracial, multi-class, and multi-accented game-lesson of my high school memories at first prevented me from understanding what I do now: that "Jabberwocky" is a ballad of the slaying of the Jabberwock, a creature "with eyes of flame" whom the child protagonist decapitates and whose head he valiantly carries out of the wood to show his proud father: "And hast thou slain the Jabberwock? / Come to my arms, my beamish boy!" Imaginary creatures called names such as "JubJub" birds and "Tumtum" trees suggest that this is not an English wood, but, perhaps, an

---

[17] The speculative is having a major moment in various fields within the humanities and some social sciences. Curious about numbers, I conducted some crude quantitative research on the matter. The program for the American Studies Association's 2022 annual meeting included more than sixty mentions of the adjective *speculative* and the verb *speculate* in more than thirty separate panels. The Association for the Study of Literature and Environment's 2021 Virtual Biennial Conference saw more than ten separate mentions of the speculative, including a special discussion on "Speculative Ecomedia." (The mentions of the term decrease with each previous program of the ASLE conference; the program for the 2015 conference included only two mentions, one of which was in the description of the plenary session by Donna Haraway and Anna Tsing. The previous two programs, 2013 and 2011, include one and zero mentions of the term, respectively.) The American Comparative Literature Association's 2022 annual meeting included eleven seminars with the speculative as a motif. The Modern Language Association's 2022 annual conference included five panels with the word *speculative* in the title and five papers with the word in the title. The 2022 National Women's Studies Association Conference included two panels dedicated to the speculative and five total mentions of the word on the program. The program for the Society for Social Studies of Science (4S) 2022 meeting included nine mentions of the word *speculative*. Finally, the 2022 History of Science Society annual meeting included only one mention.

imagined "African jungle" in some colonial outpost. That which must be slain lurks in the terrifying wilderness, a wilderness to be tamed. After all, the late nineteenth-century imaginary of the English-speaking world belonged to the Joseph Conrads and Rudyard Kiplings and the discourse of the Scramble for Africa and the Dark Continent. The playful jibberish of the "Jabberwocky" assumes a readership that would unequivocally identify with the (white male child) narrator and his father, subjects who have the capacity to rest by trees "lost in thought."

Though Haraway's "mad gardener" – who "chips," "shreds," and "layers" – echoes the character of the Hatter often recalled as the Mad Hatter, Haraway would likely not endorse Carroll's late nineteenth-century colonial message to destroy the creatures lurking in the wilderness. Instead, she promotes the integration and symbiosis with nonhuman others that, though she admits may require some destruction (of the other), differs from colonial and patriarchal destruction (Haraway 2016b: 57).[18] If the creature is to be destroyed, we must find terms that will help us reimagine the violence of the act as productive, even as a kind of "love." Recounting a discussion among colleagues about hunting and eating animals, Haraway cites her "animal rights colleague" as both acknowledging that "some hunters . . . experience and practice love for the animals they kill" and being "very glad such hunters do not love him" (Haraway 2008: 299).[19] What creatures cannot refuse this "love"? Who can both destroy *and* call it "love"?

4 The Disillusionment

4.1 A Never-ending Burial

> "It is then the black earth in which the gold or the lapis is sown like the grain of wheat. It is the black, magically fecund earth that Adam took with him from Paradise, also called antimony and described as a 'black blacker than black' (*nigrum nigrius nigro*)."
>
> Carl Jung, "Religious Ideas in Alchemy" (1937)[20]

Seduction is the game that Rose Armitage (Allison Williams) plays with Chris Washington (Daniel Kaluuya). He has become the latest in a string of black

---

[18] Haraway's writings conjure more the figure of the mad scientist than that of the mad gardener. This notion is abetted by the cover image of the paperback first edition of *Staying with the Trouble*, which is a detail from an artwork by Geraldine Gavier for her exhibit called *Playing God in an Art Lab*.

[19] Wells's *Believers* makes a similar rhetorical move: "A hunter who feels compassion for his prey might make ethical decisions about the manner and frequency of his hunts. But when, during the hunt, the hunter 'feels with' the animal, he knows on a somatic level that their subjectivities overlap, that they will be quite literally of one flesh" (Wells 2021, 155). I cannot confirm, but doubt, that the prey would wax so poetically about its demise.

[20] Jung 1995: 48–49.

boyfriends that Rose has convinced to visit her family home only to be turned into a kind of compost for the benefit of the white and white(ned) neighbors who pay for a surgical procedure that transforms them into better versions of themselves. After falling endlessly into an abyss from which he can view the world from a terrifying distance, Chris finds himself strapped into a worn, leather chair.[21] Former photographer Jim Hudson (Stephen Root), who is blind, appears on the television screen in front of Chris and cheerfully greets him. In the short conversation that follows, Chris learns that Jim's brain will be transplanted into his body while maintaining "the piece of [Chris's] brain connected to [his] nervous system" so that "those intricate connections" remain. Intensifying the horror of the fate that awaits him is that a "sliver of [Chris] will still be in there somewhere … as a passenger. An audience." Chris has already experienced what is to come when his girlfriend's mother, Missy Armitage (Catherine Keener), hypnotized him, sending him into the horrifying abyss that she calls The Sunken Place.

To proclaim that Jordan Peele's critically acclaimed blockbuster feature, *Get Out*, has become part of a popular U.S. lexicon would be an understatement. Phrases like "The Sunken Place" have entered mainstream parlance. The terror that the suburbs signify for black people – a place that has, in its inception, signified safety from black(ened) people for white and white(ned) Americans – stands out as a central motif in discussions of the movie. My reaction to the film as a horror movie echoed that of many other black viewers: this is horror insofar as living as a black person in an anti-black society is to experience life perpetually on the edge between life and violent death. When, near the end of the film, police lights flash behind Chris as he flees the Armitage property, the audience at my screening audibly groaned with the expectation that our hero would perish by cop. A police presence at the end of a horror flick often signals that the terrors experienced by the surviving characters have finally come to an end, but, here, echoing the topsy-turvy world of the black person in the United States, the police signify certain doom. When Chris's best friend Rod Williams appears on-screen in his airport security vehicle, the audience exhaled in relief.[22]

What does Peele's *Get Out* have to do with the ecological writings I discuss here? The answer is: everything and nothing. The reason for this paradox is that,

---

[21] I use the term "white(ned)" to accommodate the relative fluidity of whiteness that nevertheless remains foreclosed to most Afro-descendent people in the United States and Canada.
   My definition of "world" borrows from Tyrone Palmer's in that it is "a metonym for colonial modernity" (Palmer 2020: 253).

[22] Jordan Peele reveals that alternate endings to the film showed the cops either imprisoning Chris for the massacre of the white family or killing him on the spot for being black (Goldberg 2017).

while these writings celebrate the becoming compost, as I discuss further in what follows, they do not consider that blackness itself has been defined by being compost. Compost is an eerily apt metaphor for blackness: that which issues from death to yield life for something else. (What I call blackness as compost should not be mistaken for romanticization or a claim to a black ecology.) Chris in *Get Out* must become compost for Jim. The film adds a perverse twist to the "exchange," however, for Chris cannot completely die; he must experience his living death perpetually.

Borrowing from Cecilio Cooper's work on the black chthonic, blackness as *nigredo* is another useful metaphor. "Alchemy," writes Cooper, "speculates that celestial forces transform metal mined *underground* into superior substances topside" (Cooper 2022, emphasis added). *Nigredo*, defined as "the blackening stage of the alchemical *magnum opus*," "putrefaction," and "debasement," is the first alchemical step in creating the philosopher's stone" (Cooper 2022 and Greenberg 2000: 45 and 50). Chris, as a black(ened) person in the world, has already been identified as compost – or *nigredo* – and the brain surgery he must undergo echoes the churning and decomposition that generates compost, as well as the alchemical process that pressurizes *nigredo* into something that can generate more value. After all, Jim seeks to elevate his market value by photographing the world like talented photographer Chris, much in the same way that the philosopher's stone can be used to transform base metals into gold. Thinking of blackness as compost and *nigredo*, the Sunken Place metaphorizes a kind of never-ending burial, the forever-composting or generatively putrefy-ing quality of blackness *for* the world. According to Nathan Schwartz-Salant, the Jungian concept of *nigredo* symbolized the "dark side of the self and collective evil," whose "purpose" is to "dissolve old structures so that new ones can be created" (Schwartz-Salant 1995: 15). Far from inert, *nigredo* is a highly usable and productive idea that Carl Jung materializes as usable soil.

The productive process that requires *nigredo* before anything of more value can be made is evident in the metaphorical malleability of black suffering. Consider Chilean poet-artist Cecilia Vicuña's review of Tobago-Canadian poet M. Nourbese Philip's *Zong!* This book-length poem, an abstracted retelling of the unimaginable violence of the murder by drowning of 150 enslaved Africans in exchange for insurance money, becomes the *nigredo* from which Vicuña's horizontal relationality can grow. "I read M. Nourbese Philip's *Zong!* (2008) not as the song of the drowned slaves but the song of all of us, who are now becoming slaves, albeit by other names, on the slave ship Earth" (Vicuña 2019). So opens Vicuña's review of the poem for *Frieze* magazine. To under-stand fully, in this case, is to subsume, consume, and overtake. The enslaved African, murdered for insurance, has no claim to injury. Trapped in a perpetual

Sunken Place, where his or her cries, even when heard, will not be discerned, and even when discerned, will have the use-value of fueling a becoming for the *poiesis* of the non-black being who wonders: "How is the court language that calls the slaves 'property' different from the language that calls corporations 'people'?" (Vicuña 2019). Here, in evidence, is the failure of language in elucidating black suffering, an idea that Philip's poem explores. Some ecological writings invoke a "we" that, with disturbing frequency, replaces an insight emergent specifically from a black experience of the world. In Vicuña's review, a poem dedicated precisely to the failure of language in relation to the tortures of the Middle Passage becomes compost or *nigredo* for its claim that "we are all slaves" (Vicuña 2019).

The basic problem of this "we" and its expected relationality when we consider racialization, and specifically (anti-)blackness, is that all "humans" have not existed, lived, or died on a flat horizontal plane. For Haraway, the "we" is instrumentalized against the Western subject's "I": "Since I am a moralist, the real question must have more virtue: who are 'we'?" Haraway acknowledges that this question is "always ready for contingent, friction-generating articulations," a statement that gives room both to her conception of "we" and to the potential absorption of critique as creating generative friction. I follow the work of black critical thinker and philosopher Axelle Karera in pressuring ecological writers' concept of the "we." One of Karera's interventions is to name what she considers to be the two "insidious discursive inclinations" of Anthropocene discourse and its resounding "erasure of race": first, "the naturalization of relationality, mutual dependency, and other narratives of 'species entanglements,'" and, second, "an ahistorical and apolitical 'hyper-valuation' of the concept of life" (Karera 2019: 34). Karera cautions against these Anthropocene narratives' "generalized – perhaps even calculated – unwillingness to account for past and current imperial injustices, coupled with a rampant inability to imagine alternative futures outside an apocalyptic state of emergency that is mostly inspired by a narrative of vitality, and in which disposable life or 'life-death' remains largely unaccounted for" (Karera 2019: 33). Extraction and allocation of resources have not been evenly meted out and, as such, pronouncements to acknowledge that "we," humans and nonhumans alike, are "all" interwoven in processes of becoming and unbecoming, without attention to how these differences reify these inequities. Though Haraway, Wells, and Allewaert all make a version of the argument that "we" are "all" compost, I argue that, in fact, we have *not all* been positioned as such (Haraway 2016b: 101; Wells 2021b; and Allewaert 2013: 17). As a tentative correlative, Karera suggests considering "an ethics based on the radically non-relational" (Karera 2019: 47–48).

Relationalists obscure that what looks like relation from one perspective is parasitism from another. In this parasitic relationship between the non-black subject and the black or black(ened) position, the parasitism is sublimated. Denise Ferreira da Silva, for instance, argues that "the economic relationship" between enslaved black labor and the present-day economic world order has been occluded and erased (Ferreira da Silva 2014: 83). To Frank B. Wilderson III, "cinematic and political discourse since the 1980s, tend to hide rather than make explicit the grammar of suffering which underwrites the United States and its foundational antagonisms" (Wilderson 2010: 6). After all, "grammar is assumed" and "unspoken," but nevertheless structuring (Wilderson 2010: 5).

Haraway's writings get close to suggesting that the "we" operative in them may not include black people. In endnotes scattered throughout this oeuvre, blackness manifests as a wrinkle in theories of human–nonhuman relations. (As she herself describes it, endnotes allow Haraway to "sin," where she "yields" to the "temptation" to say what she senses she either should not say or would throw a wrench at the fast-speeding generative train in the body of the text [Haraway 1991: 334n28].[23]) This wrinkle does not significantly reshape the writings about human–nonhuman relations except to repeatedly inspire the metaphor of pregnancy and biological symbiosis, as I discuss in what follows. In one such endnote, Haraway condemns a "viciously racist image" targeted to doctors, concluding that "black women do not have the *discursive* status of woman/human in white culture" (Haraway 1991: 334n26).[24] Given this acknowledgment of black women's discursive difference from women and other humans in "white culture," how is one to read Haraway's analyses of the human throughout her writings? Is the assumption that Haraway's work, unlike the work of the white male thinkers she unflinchingly skewers, operates in a culture outside of whiteness? Haraway points toward "the abject failure of the social studies of science as an organized discourse to take account of the last twenty years of feminist inquiry" (Haraway 1991: 332). One could argue that she also stalls when it comes to absorbing the lessons of black critical thought and black feminism and, instead, turns her critical gaze toward the feminisms – white and "transnational" – that repeatedly cannot account for black women's differential or non-humanness. Haraway lists the "histories of colonialism, racism, sexism, and class domination" as having created the kinds of binaries she cautions against and which she ascribes to a white patriarchal imaginary that

---

[23] Another essay points out Haraway's propensity to relegate to endnotes her discussions of how blackness, black history, and black people connect to her broader frameworks (Davis et al. 2019: 5).

[24] See also Haraway 1991: 308.

presumes the wholeness of "One" (Haraway 1991: 296).[25] However, simply naming "racism" as a problem is not the same as allowing it to transform one's thinking. When it comes to blackness, Haraway's writings repeatedly encounters an epistemic wall, a point beyond which they seem unable to go.[26] This has not only to do with whiteness, but also with disciplinarity and training, as well as their interrelationship.

Despite their "interdisciplinarity," Haraway's methods and ethics are in the service of science-as-expertise with humanistic methods as vehicles for pathos and storytelling.[27] Language – and stories – decorate science-driven, positivist inquiry. Myriad examples throughout her oeuvre reveal what the sign of "interdisciplinarity" serves both for her scholarship and for the demands of the neoliberal US university. For instance, *Primate Visions* makes a confounding set of equivalences in the following passage: "Wage labor, sexual and reproductive appropriation, and racial hegemony are structured aspects of the human world. There is no doubt that they affect knowledge systematically, but it is not clear precisely how they relate to knowledge about feeding patterns of patas monkeys or about the replication of DNA molecules" (Haraway 1989: 7). One could, of course, also state that the feeding patterns of patas monkeys would not tell us anything about wage labor. Though the purpose of this comparative list is unclear, especially when *Primate Visions* has nothing to do with patas monkeys or DNA molecules, it exemplifies the flippancy with which systems of extraction and exploitation emerge in Haraway's work.

Years later, Haraway shared her sheepish encounters with primatologists, who apparently felt insulted by her portrayals of the field in *Primate Visions*. She told her interviewer that she felt the need to clarify to them and in the rest of her work just how much she respected them (Haraway and Nichols Goodeve 2000: 56–57). The same vigorous shame does not surge, however, when critiques are launched from various fields of the humanities and social sciences. Indeed, Haraway's responses to these critiques can be characterized as impatient. For instance, in her response to two reviews of her concept of "Making Kin, Not Babies," including a particularly critical one by Jade S. Sasser, whose work on reproductive justice and the environment is attentive to race, Haraway writes:

---

[25] She calls some of these white male thinkers "adolescent boys" and criticizes what she calls "masculinist self-birthing" (Haraway 1991: 299 and 336n38). See also Haraway 1981 and Haraway 2008: 319n51.

[26] For more on the limitations of white feminism in relation to blackness, see Wilderson 2010: 135–137. For more on the limitations of white feminism in relation to non-white and colonized positions, see Spivak 1999.

[27] Haraway's doctorate is in biology (Haraway and Nichols Goodeve 2000: 132).

> I have little sympathy for what I experience as a taboo in progressive thinking, including feminist, antiracist, decolonial, reproductive thinking, which seems to hold that practically any topic or category can be brought into intersectional work on generations and reproduction *except* counting increasing and decreasing human numbers, no matter how nuanced, situated, and attentive to violence. What I want is a different demography, one that worries about how, when, and if to count human beings in entangled living and dying with microbes, plants, animals, and apparatuses, and one that asks about numbers-in-worlds from non-Malthusian foundations. I am not interested in starting from comparative birth, death, and growth rates of the eaters and the eaten. I want a radical, nonhumanist demography embedded in multi-kinded/ multi-species justice and care. (Strathern et al. 2019: 170)[28]

I cite this passage at length not only because one wonders to whom this passage refers as the "eaters" and the "eaten," but also because it is instructive to see the logic it follows as it dismisses questions of inequality and representation. The reasoning here is that systemic inequality is a "mere" human matter. The impatience with questions of human justice – which are, to me, inseparable from environmental and animal justice – evident in this passage, stems more from the inability of critical feminist and gender studies, as well as studies attentive to racial injustice, to offer practical help with the forms of material-semiotic *tinkering* that Haraway's work – and the work of many other thinkers inspired by climate change – considers instrumental to stall ecological collapse. It is worthwhile to note that the nonscientists and nonphilosophers of science who emerge as inspiring in Haraway's writings are the science fiction writer Octavia Butler and the painter Lynn Randolph, whose works give linguistic and visual *materia prima* for speculative tinkering. These passages also inspire doubt about just how interdisciplinary Haraway's celebrated "interdisciplinarity" truly is.

Blackness – which is not reducible to though it does forcibly, historically intersect with African or Afro-descendent ethnicities and cultures – is here defined as being in the structural position of extractability for others' benefit. A long history of black writing elaborates some form of this argument, including Eric William's *Capitalism and Slavery*, Aimé Césaire's *Discourse on Colonialism*, Toni Morrison's *Playing in the Dark: Whiteness and the Literary Imagination*, Saidiya Hartman's *Scenes of Subjection: Terror, Slavery, and Self-Making in Nineteenth-Century America*, Frank B. Wilderson III's *Red, White, & Black: Cinema and the Structures of U.S. Antagonisms*, Denise Ferreira da Silva's "Toward a Black Feminist Poethics," Calvin Warren's *Ontological Terror: Blackness, Nihilism, and Emancipation*, Zakiyyah Iman Jackson's *Becoming*

---

[28] *Making Kin, Not Population* is an anthology of essays that respond to Haraway's concept of "Making Kin, Not Babies."

Human: Matter and Meaning in an Anti-Black World, and Selamawit D. Terrefe's "The Pornotrope of Decolonial Feminism." In his 1944 economic study *Capitalism and Slavery*, Williams centralizes "the role of Negro slavery and the slave trade in providing the capital which financed the Industrial Revolution in England" (Williams 1944, vii). Eleven years later, Césaire uses the adjective "plundering" to describe colonialism and decries the extent to which Western or European fields of knowledge exist to rationalize – through "false objectivity" – this parasitic relationship (Césaire 2000: 55 and 56).[29] Hartman argues how "the texture of freedom is laden with the vestiges of slavery . . . and abstract equality is utterly enmeshed in the narrative of black subjection" (Hartman 1997, 116). Morrison's long essay on canonical US literatures "contemplate[s] how Africanist personae, narrative, and idiom moved and enriched the text in self-conscious ways, to consider what the engagement meant for the work of the [white US] writer's imagination" (Morrison 1992: 16). Wilderson analyzes late twentieth-century US films through the contention that "the imaginary of the state and civil society is parasitic on the Middle Passage" and "the structure of the entire world's semantic field . . . is sutured by anti-black solidarity" (Wilderson 2010: 11 and 58). Moreover, he argues for the centrality of the symbolic, over the economic, benefits to the state and civil society in the enslavement of black people over the enslavement of Europeans and their descendants, considering the latter would have made more economic sense (Wilderson 2010: 13–15). For her part, Ferreira da Silva demonstrates that "the total value produced by slave labor continues to sustain global capital" (Ferreira da Silva 2014, 82). In his metaphysical exploration of blackness and anti-blackness, Warren insists that "Blacks . . . have function but not Being – the function of black(ness) is to give form to a terrifying formlessness (nothing)" (Warren 2018: 5). Moreover, he contends that "anti-black violence is violence against nothing, the nothing that unsettles the human because it can never be captured and dominated" (Warren 2018: 21). Jackson asks, "what is the being of blackness?" and answers, in part, that "it is an essential enabling condition for something of, but distinguishable from, its source – and therefore, it performs a kind of natality, performing a *generative* function rather than serving as an identity" (Jackson 2020: 69, emphasis added). Finally, Terrefe closely reads the work of decolonial feminist María Lugones and finds, in part, the "rhetorical use of Black American women" (Terrefe 2020: 135).

My thinking with these varied scholars does not suggest that they all make the same or even similar arguments, or that they have the same goals in advancing

---

[29] Césaire also provides the example of Belgian colonialism: "Let them plunder and torture in the Congo, let the Belgian colonizer seize all the natural resources" (Césaire 2000: 57–58).

them; indeed, placed in conversation with one another, these texts would disagree on important claims. My aim with this list is to highlight that these texts all explore how the Western world as a whole or in parts has relied, in some form, both on extractions from black people themselves – in their labor, cultures, reproduction, sexuality, and so on – and blackness as a figure, position, or non-place.

After Chris asks, "Why us? . . . Why black people?" Jim laughs and responds: "Who knows? People want to change. Some people want to be stronger, faster, cooler. But don't . . . please don't lump me in with that. You know, I could give a shit what, what color you are. No. What I want is deeper. I want your eye, man. I want those things you see through." Horrified and incredulous, Chris says, "this is crazy." Looking away from the camera and from Chris, Jim tells someone off-screen: "Okay, I'm done." I recount this exchange because several elements are crucial to some of what I am arguing in this essay. First, Jim denies knowing "why black people" are chosen to be carapaces for white people's attainment of strength, speed, and ineffable cool. Second, Jim refuses being associated with the other whites performing this symbiotic "exchange"; he argues that he sees beyond Jim's skin color – that is, his blackness – to extract something "deeper." However, his desire for Chris's "eyes," or his view of the world, is undeniably tied to his experience of the world as a black man. Jim desires the glory of Chris's talent for photography without the painful history attendant to it. Finally, Jim seeks absolution from being associated with violent whiteness while demonstrating that he does not care how Chris feels about his fate. The film skewers a white liberal relationship to blackness that both relies on blackness as compost and desires absolution for the violence it requires to maintain itself.

In *Staying with the Trouble*, Haraway declares: "I am a compostist, not a posthumanist: we are all compost, not posthuman" (Haraway 2016b: 101). "The edge of extinction," she continues, "is not just a metaphor; system collapse is not a thriller. Ask any refugee of any species" (Haraway 2016b: 101–102). So starts the narrative of what "we" must urgently do if "we" are to keep human population numbers and myriad forms of life-ending destruction at bay. To imagine what else could be, Haraway shares a "collective speculative fabulation" in the last chapter of *Staying with the Trouble,* called "The Camille Stories: Children of Compost" (Haraway 2016b: 8). The speculative fabulation "follows five generations of a symbiogenetic join of a human child and monarch butterflies along the many lines and nodes of these insects' migrations between Mexico and the United States and Canada. These lines trace socialities and materialities crucial to living and dying with critters on the edge of disappearance so that they might go on" (Haraway 2016b: 8).

"The Camille Stories" emerged from a workshop on speculative narration that Haraway had attended. There, small groups of two or three people were tasked with "fabulating a baby, and somehow bringing the infant through five human generations" (Haraway 2016b: 134). Her group, which included filmmaker Fabrizio Terranova and philosopher-scientist Vinciane Despret, came up with the story of the Camilles, who were to be part of the Children of Compost community. Their group set out to "radically reduce the pressure of human numbers on earth, currently set on a course to climb to more than 11 billion by the end of the twenty-first century CE" (Haraway 2016b: 136–137). Starting in 2025, with Camille 1, and ending in 2425, with Camille 5, the Children of the Compost, even five generations later, are "not yet able to fill the obligations that the Haudenosaunee Confederacy imposed on themselves and so on anyone who has been touched by the account, even in acts of unacknowledged appropriation, namely, to act so as to be response-able to and for those in the seventh generation to come" (Haraway 2016b: 144). Nevertheless, over these "five generations, the total number of human beings on earth, including persons in symbiosis with vulnerable animals chosen by their birth parent (syms) and those not in such symbioses (non-syms), declined from the high point of 10 billion in 2100 to a stable level of 3 billion by 2400" (Haraway 2016b: 144). In Haraway's definition, "symbiont and symbiote ... both refer to an organism living in a state of symbiosis, *whether beneficial to one or both (or more) or not* ... Symbiogenesis refers to the cobbling together of living entities to make something new in the biological, rather than digital or some other, mode" (Haraway 2016b: 218n8, emphasis added).

Haraway tries to forestall the critique that the violence of drastic population control has always been unevenly meted out with references to urgent endings heralding new beginnings. She narrates the years after Camille 1 as one of "radical collective action" that "could ferment a turbulent but generative time of reversals, revolt, revolution, and resurgence" (Haraway 2016b: 145). Haraway describes her storytelling "as full of dying as living, as full of endings, even genocides, as beginnings" (Haraway 2016b: 10). An endnote admits that "the process of rebalancing and human reduction without exacerbating deep inequalities was difficult in every imaginable way across the earth" (Haraway 2016b: 217n7). Although "coercion to make or not make a new child was considered a crime and could result in banishment from the community ... sometimes violent conflict over bringing new babies into existence or over determining who and what were kin did occur" (Haraway 2016b: 217n7). Moreover, "it never stopped being necessary to oppose oppressive and totalitarian forces in the intentional communities, just as it never ceased to be necessary to interrogate the discursive categories marked by 'bio-' that informed symbiogenesis" (Haraway 2016b: 218n7). In other words, the defining struggle of who gets to live full and healthy lives with loved ones and who does not remains an equally salient debate in the world that Haraway, Terranova, and Despret fabulate. The stakes seem to be population control for the sake of perpetuating some forms of life, specifically, the lives of those in the Children of the Compost communities, which can be found all over the world except Africa and the Caribbean, in symbiosis with chosen, nonhuman species.[30] Srinivas Aravamudan critically highlights "the quasi-Nazi propositions of deep ecology" in which "long-term species survival means radical reduction of the population" (Aravamudan 2013: 23).[31] But it is not the survival of these nonhuman "critters" that seems to be the point, for, even in this speculative fabulation, the monarch butterflies chosen as the symbiont for the Camilles become extinct by the era of Camille 5. Thus, the stakes of this imagined "otherwise" world seem to be to perpetuate white(ned) life under the new banner of the multispecies/miscegenated, white *indigène*.[32]

(Non-African) Indigenous communities surface in the Camille Stories as wise and compliant guides into and within this "otherwise" world. "Camille 1," for instance, "had studied with Native American, First Nation, and Métis teachers, who explained and performed diverse practices and knowledges for conjoined human and other-than-human becoming and exchange" (Haraway 2016b: 153). For Camille 2, "the Mazahuas of central Mexico ... became vital" (Haraway 2016b: 154). These Indigenous people "took her in hand" in their practice of "vigorous nonviolence," which Haraway names "the Zapatistas' most important contribution," in contrast with their "transformative armed uprising in Chiapas" in 1994 (Haraway 2016b: 155). In this telling, the Zapatista strategy moves from rage (armed uprising) to love

---

[30] The places that Haraway lists as hosting "some of the other settlements and migrations of the Communities of Compost" are China ("led by older rural women and Chinese Green movement activists"), Canada (led "by indigenous and southern coalitions"), Australia ("in solidarity with Wangan and Jagalingou peoples' resistance to a Carmichael coal mine"), "the Navajo and Hopi nations on Black Mesa, in alliance with Anglo, Latino, and native activists," Peru, and Bolivia (Haraway 2016b: 217n6).

[31] It is unclear whether Aravamudan would place Haraway's work in this vein, for his essay, though critical of "climate change criticism," ends with a consideration of the possibilities in Deleuzian and Latourian thought in ways that also recall Haraway's thought.

[32] "Otherwise" has recently become an important keyword within some areas of black studies, especially in relation to black ecology, spirituality, and vitalism, and as it intersects with North American Native studies. For a critique of the "otherwise" in black studies, see Palmer 2020. For a critique of the Henri Bergsonian and other, at times fascistic, vitalisms that seduced *négritude* poets, see Jones 2010. A strand in present-day black studies is taken with vitalism, especially in reaction to afropessimistic and otherwise unflinching analyses of anti-blackness. Of concern here is not well-researched work on how black culture and sociality thrive in spite of the world's anti-blackness (this is usually the focus of my work); of concern here is how black culture and sociality are weaponized to silence scholarship on anti-blackness.

(nonviolence), echoing Haraway's description of her own scholarly transformation, as I discuss later in this Element. In another geography, Haraway mentions the "Community of Compost in Amazonian Peru [that] was especially attuned to the local butterflies, who sip the tears of turtles for vital minerals" as an example of "indigenous cosmopolitics" (Haraway 2016b: 227n41).

Haraway admits that unequally meted out violence is unavoidable in the attempts to curtail the growth of the global human population, "as it always had," but does not delve into what this entails (Haraway 2016b: 217n7).[33] This violence includes the history of forced sterilizations especially of non-white women, the removal from their families of Indigenous children throughout the colonized world (including African children on their way to enslavement throughout the Western world), and the ongoing historical denial of motherhood to black women from slavery to the present day. Haraway's concept of making "oddkin" emerges as one of her neologisms, celebrated in a bumper sticker that exclaims "Make Kin, Not Babies" and defined by "three-or-more parent practices" that were "pro child, proparent, pro friendship, and pro community, for human people and other critters alike," and in which "making kin" was a "sympoetic" rather than "biogenetic" endeavor (Haraway 2016b: 220–221n17). Though the practices of non-African Indigenous communities frequently appear as "inspirations" for how to live, unmentioned here is that a defining component of black cultures in the Americas was the making of kinship structures over and over again, in the face of relentless destruction and shortened life.[34]

4.2 The Scraping of History

The replacement of seminal, patriarchal, and phallic genealogy with maternal, rhizomic, and horizontal relationality emerges as a central procedure in Haraway's *Primate Visions*. This long book aims to "be responsible to primatologists, to historians of science, to cultural theorists, to the broad left, anti-racist, anti-colonial, and women's movements, to animals, and to lovers of serious stories" (Haraway 1989: 3). *Primate Visions* focuses on twentieth-century primatology, Africa, and specifically (white) primatologists' visions and manipulations of Africa and African people.[35] Various examples show how

---

[33] For another example of where violence emerges as inevitable in Haraway's speculative fabulation, see Haraway 2016b: 140.

[34] Haraway gestures toward this history in an interview after *Staying with the Trouble*'s publication when she says: "I think LGBTQI people from all sections of society, as well as many Indigenous Peoples and African-American communities, have been the most innovative in the United States in terms of building and sustaining really interesting kinds of kin networks, often against great odds" (Paulson 2019).

[35] *Primate Visions* also includes a short section on Japanese primatology. I do not delve into this component not because it is entirely irrelevant, but because, as Haraway herself concedes, the relevant historical stakes, though intersecting, differ.

white men's hunting of African "big game" at the turn of the twentieth century exemplified the seminal nature of the white patriarchal scientific model "that turns everything into a resource for appropriation" (Haraway 1989: 13). Moreover, "as 'resource' an object of knowledge is finally only matter for the seminal power, the act, of the knower" (Haraway 1989: 13). The book then argues that white female primatologists were enlisted to become white male hunter's "surrogates" in a decolonizing Africa (Haraway 1989: 152). In an astute analysis of how race, gender, and colonialism coalesced, the book asserts that white men were "being thrown out of the garden [i.e., colonized Africa] by decolonization and perhaps off the planet by its destruction in ecological devastation and nuclear holocaust" (Haraway 1989: 152). The exclusion is not complete, for "whiteness must be attended to, if the re-entry of the west into Africa at the moment of decolonization is to be narrated" (Haraway 1989: 152). So enters "the blond and white female mediator to negotiate the discourses of exterminism and extinction in space and the jungle" (Haraway 1989: 152). According to Haraway's analysis of this shift from the while male hunter to the white female scientist, the white female scientist is absolved of colonialism and is instead a "surrogate" in search of "touch" from "the animals [that] are [themselves] (colored) surrogates for all who have been colonized in the name of nature and whose judgement can no longer be repressed" (Haraway 1989: 152). The book's tracing of how the white male hunter/taxidermist/museum researcher comes to be discursively – if not also literally – replaced by the white female scientist/lab researcher/conservationist is an incisive observation. However, this tracing, which acknowledges that white women replaced white men by "softening" the violence of extraction in Africa, is followed by an *avowal* (not merely ambivalence) of these white women scientists' surrogacy in its celebration of their innovative, feminist scientific methods. Excepting Jane Goodall, skewered in *Primate Visions*, these white women primatologists' methods would inspire Haraway's method and ethics of "curiosity" in several of her subsequent works. In what follows, I delve into this and the other optimistic and positivist methods that emerge in Haraway's writings, including "politeness," "love," and "care."

Though *Primate Visions* is a complex exploration of the relationship between scientific knowledge about primates and colonialism, in *When Species Meet*, Haraway would chastise herself for having "failed the obligation of curiosity" in that earlier book (Haraway 2008: 312n29). In other words, Haraway's implied critique of how these white women primatologists reinstated a colonial and extractive system of thought would, years later, signal incuriosity from her shifted perspective. If *Primate Visions* was written with rage, as Haraway says was the case for "A Cyborg Manifesto," written in the same years as *Primate Visions*, an association between rage and incuriosity – as well as with the procedures of deconstructive critique – help define the shift in her methods (Haraway and Nichols Goodeve 2000: 54).[36] Haraway contrasts this "rage" with what she calls "love" and "curiosity." The implication is that critique-as-such is *not* loving, *not* curious, and certainly *not* generative. In an interview, Haraway states that she "hates" the "model" of critique that searches for what is not in the text (akin to paranoid critique) or for the text's shortcomings. Haraway considers this form of critique particularly noxious when it comes to "racism." She states:

> You can't do away with racisms by various kinds of mantras or by pointing out how this article didn't deal with race in such a such a way [*sic*] and then sit back and think look how I'm free because I noticed … It isn't only white people who have this relationship to racism. And I think some of this style of negative criticality in graduate school in relation, not just to racism but many other kinds of things, is rooted in a fear of embracing some thing with all of its messiness and dirtiness and imperfection. (Haraway and Nichols Goodeve 2000: 111–112)

Her interviewer describes Haraway's anti-critical approach as "generative criticality" (Haraway and Nichols Goodeve 2000: 114).

At the end of *Primate Visions*, the grammar of black suffering is enlisted to help generate possibilities of future becoming. Instead of the game of replacements and surrogacies between white patriarchs and their white proverbial daughters in the field, the text unironically suggests "miscegenation" as the solution to the problem of the patriarchal replication of the One. The case is made through a reading of Octavia Butler's Xenogenesis series, starting with *Dawn* (1987). Haraway grants that these stories of "miscegenation," this time between a human and an extraterrestrial species rather than between white and black humans, are "deeply informed by Afro-American perspectives with strong tones of womanism or feminism" (Haraway 1989: 378). Haraway notes that the narrative "begins not with the white girl child brought to Africa, but with the black woman taken out, who seeds the diaspora that stands as a figure of this history and possible future of a very polymorphous species" (Haraway 1989: 378). Moreover, she describes the novel as a "survival story" rather than a "salvation history," defined greatly by "mutation, metamorphosis, and diaspora" rather than "origins" which are "precisely that to which Butler's people [i.e., black people] do not have access" (Haraway 1989: 378).

---

[36] Another apt example of Haraway's early-career critical method can be found in her essay "In the Beginning Was the Word: The Genesis of Biological Theory," which does not shy away from strongly critiquing various new works in science studies, broadly defined (Haraway 1981). (Coincidentally, one of the epigraphs to that essay is a quote from Lewis Carroll's *Through the Looking Glass*.)

The extraterrestrial Other, the Oankali, are in the position of power in this series, and they "rescue" humans under coercive conditions. In Haraway's retelling, the Oankali "are ... fascinated by Lilith's [the black protagonist] 'talent' for cancer, which killed several of her relatives, but which in Oankali 'hands' would become a technology for regeneration and metamorphosis" (Haraway 1989: 380). Extracting regenerative value from murderous cancer cells is not enough for the Oankali, who "want more from humanity; they want a full trade, which will require the intimacies of sexual mingling and embodied pregnancy in a shared colonial venture in, of all places, the Amazon valley" (Haraway 1989: 380). Because "pregnancy raises the tricky question of consent, property in the self, and the humans' love of themselves as the sacred image, the sign of the same," Haraway has "always preferred the prospect of pregnancy with the embryo of another species" (Haraway 1989: 377). In other words, Haraway equates Lilith's recoil from being forcibly impregnated by the Oankali with white patriarchs' narcissistic humanity. Earlier in *Primate Visions*, Haraway suggests that "total death" would yield neither knowledge nor pregnancy. That is, the physical death of an entity does not necessarily lead to "total death." This is because "scientific knowledge," she writes, "canceled death; only death before knowledge was final, an abortive act in the natural history of progress" (Haraway 1989: 34). In the context of *Primate Visions*, this statement critiques hunter-taxidermist Carl Akeley's attempt to revamp himself into a conservationist. However, considered alongside her reading of Butler's novel and its narrative of forced pregnancy, I detect that, in Haraway's logic, scientific knowledge is a form of vitalist instrumentalization of certain forms of destruction. Even when there is destruction, in this case the violation of a black woman who neither wants a pregnancy nor to die of cancer, the ending of *Primate Visions* intimates that these exchanges are, in some way, productive of knowledge for the Oankali or of biological becoming-with the Oankali, and, as such, are the science that can give life to death. The destruction and death – of some – thus become generative.

Staying with the Trouble reads as the resolution of what in *Primate Visions* remained a fraught space of inquiry. *Primate Visions* concludes that

> the terms for gestating the term of future worlds constitute a defining dilemma of reproductive politics. The contending shapes of sameness and difference in any possible future are at stake in the primate order's unfinished narrative of traffic across the specific cultural and political boundaries that separate and link animal, human, and machine in a contemporary global world where survival is at stake. Finally, this contested world is the primate field where, *with or without our consent*, we are located. (Haraway 1989: 382, emphasis added)

What Haraway later claims as the "incuriosity" of *Primate Visions* becomes the insight of *Staying with the Trouble*: the symbiotic joining of human and nonhuman species for human survival (as I noted, the monarch butterflies become extinct after a few generations of the experiment). However, this insight is blind to the violence it regurgitates from *Primate Visions*. If "we" are all "located," "with or without our consent," "in the "primate field," then black women's specific claims to bodily autonomy cease to matter very much. As the urgency of the end of the world beckons, questions of coercion, history, and violence increasingly diminish in importance through this weaponized "we."

I ponder the scripting of a history of enslaved black women's rape as a site of possibility and futurity *for all* – "where survival is at stake" – when enslaved black women's rape was profitable precisely to the white patriarchal property owner that Haraway subtly associates with Lilith's desire to be in charge of her own body. (Butler's own scripting of Lilith's journey remains more ambivalent than Haraway's reimagining of it as containing inspiring futurities.) The rape of black women, and the resulting coerced pregnancies, were not only reproductive in a biological sense but also productive and profitable as reproduction neatly grew the property holdings of the owner. The impunity of these violations, and the resulting growth of property *for some*, only served to further bind whiteness with property and impunity, and blackness with function, matter-for-use, and inherent vice and criminality. This cooption of coerced reproduction as a site of humanity's and the planet's ecosystem's salvation relies on blackness as compost. While the site of inspiration as having been the forcibly impregnated black woman disappears, Haraway's keen focus on pregnancy remains surprisingly present considering her insistence that human population control is crucial to preventing further ecological collapse. By the time of the publication of *Staying with the Trouble*, published almost three decades after *Primate Visions*, it seems that the world's end is too urgent to dwell on questions of consent and force. "Turn[ing]" on "figures of pregnancy and gestation," Haraway "displace[s] the terminology of reproduction with that of generation. Very rarely does anything really get reproduced; what's going on is much more polymorphous than that … And best of all, 'reproduction' – or less inaccurately, the generation of novel forms – need not be imagined in the stodgy bipolar terms of hominids" (Haraway 1991: 299). The "prized touch" between human and animal that Haraway argues white women primatologists enacted in decolonizing Africa becomes a more complete union of two entities through (forced) hybrid pregnancy. This story of forced hybrid pregnancy then becomes the somewhat sublimated basis of Haraway's exploration of sympoesis and symbiosis.

4.3 Curiosity and "Love" Killed the Cat

In this section, I delve into how Haraway's methods of curiosity, love, politeness, and rewriting intertwine to create a larger ethics of forced relationality and against the kind of critique that would slow or forestall the force of relation. I do so by focusing on instances where her writings delve into her varied inspirations, including Vinciane Despret, her sportswriter father, bioanthropologist/primatologist Barbara Smuts, and the world of science fiction.

To fully understand how relationality emerges in Haraway's writings, I will first make a detour into her defense of the usage of lab animals. She maintains that "work, use, and instrumentality are intrinsic to bodily webbed mortal earthly being and becoming," and, as such, lab animals cannot be conceived as "victims" or "other to the human" and their deaths as "sacrifice" (Haraway 2008: 71 and 74). Haraway "resist[s] the tendency to condemn all relations of instrumentality between animals and people as necessarily involving objectification and oppression of a kind similar to [those] of sexism, colonialism, and racism" (Haraway 2008: 73 and 74). Rather, using a fascinating oxymoron, she describes lab animals as "significantly unfree partners" (Haraway 2008: 74). Haraway quotes from an email from fellow scholar of ecology and extinction Thom van Dooren, who questions her approach to the "work" of lab animals:

> How might we actually inhabit a shared space of suffering with them [lab animals], and to what end? Especially when so much of this suffering seems completely unjustified and preventable ... I'm not sure what solidarity and sharing amount to unless I'm willing to take their place. Which prompts a whole lot of questions about why I can't switch places with them, why, for example, some creatures (even some humans) are "allowed" to suffer and others are not. (cited in Haraway 2008: 331n5)

Swerving out of direct line of questioning of uneven suffering, Haraway points the finger at critique: "in view of the terrible similarities [between the suffering of lab animals and the suffering of some humans], *too much sway has been given to critique* and not enough to seeing what else is going on in instrumental human-animal world makings and what else is needed" (Haraway 2008: 74, emphasis added). Far from recoiling from the potential charge of humans' instrumentalization of animal or sub/some human lives for human ends, she declares that "relations of use are exactly what companion species are all about" (Haraway 2008: 74). By describing these "partners" and "companions" as "unfree," she acknowledges that "real pain, physical and mental, including a great deal of killing, is often directly caused by the instrumental apparatus, and the pain is not borne symmetrically" (Haraway 2008: 72 and 74). Rather than condemning the use of lab animals, she insists that some acts of suffering and killing in the lab are "thoroughly justified" and that "these practices should never leave their practitioners in moral comfort" (Haraway 2008: 75).

Following this logic, only two positions seem possible: one that justifies, in the name of science-as-speculative fabulation animal experimentation as "moral" or "righteous" and another that "cultur[es] a *radical* ability to remember and feel what is going on and performing the epistemological, emotional, and technical work to respond practically in the face of permanent complexity not resolved by taxonomic hierarchies and with no humanist philosophical or religious guarantees" (Haraway 2008: 75, emphasis added). She calls "human beings' learning to share other animals' pain nonmimetically" not only an "ethical obligation, a practical problem, and an ontological opening," but also "a love that escapes calculation but requires the invention of speculative thought" (Haraway 2008: 84 and 85). Although she would not "deny the importance of the question of animals' suffering and the criminal disregard of it throughout human orders," Haraway does not "think that is the decisive question, the one that turns the order of things around, the one that promises an autre-mondialisation" (Haraway 2008: 22). Science and the speculative thought that fabulates alternative worlds trump unequal suffering – what the text truncates as "pity" – with the "promise" contained in the questions such as: "Can animals play? Or work?" (Haraway 2008: 22)

In Haraway's ecological writings, everything is always already relational and everything is in the process of becoming: "You don't have units plus relations. You just have relations. You have worlding. The whole story is about *gerunds* – worlding, bodying, everything-ing" (Weigel 2019). At the same time, because these writings also grant that some parts of the entities in relation to each other must be destroyed or sacrificed in this process, I wondered what kind of scholarly and ethical method abets the argument for forced interspecies relationality. Thangam Ravindranathan's review of various of Haraway's works describes her method as guided by "the resolute preference for love/joy/rage over critique, for stories over theories, for messy multiplicities over neatness is in turn of a piece with an overall poetic and ethical sensibility that runs deep" (Ravindranathan 2018). I would argue that Haraway associates "rage" with her earlier writings and "love" with her more recent, and "poetical," oeuvre (Ravindranathan 2018). In Haraway's method, "addition not subtraction" becomes a mantra (Weigel 2019).[37] One reading of this tendency traces it to Haraway's activism;

---

[37] As Rey Chow notes, this additive propensity is part and parcel of the anti-critical stance writ large. Bruno Latour, she writes, "equates critique with a taking away (a subtraction from reality) and advocates in its stead an adding-to" and "[Eve] Sedgewick speaks of adding, of assembling, and of conferring plenitude on an object" (Chow 2021: 11 and 13).

"enlarging the litter" of "allies" to block a perceived larger enemy is more important than "insist[ing] on a stronger [critical] apparatus" (Weigel 2019). This activist approach to thought, however, delimits intellectual inquiry. To insist that intellectual work is always political, even when it purports to be apolitical, is not synonymous with assuming that all worthy scholarship should be written by practicing "scholar activists," or that scholarship has the use-value of making policies and other action points, especially as defined by US liberals. A bigger problem with the stance that one should push aside differences to build larger coalitions of "allies" is that not everyone agrees on what constitutes an ally. In Haraway's writings frequently emerges an allyship or a "we" that is constituted by a broadly understood feminist, anti-racist, environmentally responsible left. As scholars such as Frank B. Wilderson III and Rei Terada have differently argued, however, these kinds of coalitions or associations with the radical left cannot escape the anti-black underpinnings of the Western episteme to which they belong (Wilderson 2010 and Terada 2019).

In a 2019 interview, Haraway explains that her "interest . . . in words and the sensuality of words" was influenced by her sportswriter father's disinterest in writing "critical pieces exposing the industry's financial corruption or what have you" to focus instead on telling and writing presumably uncritical stories (Weigel 2019). Haraway frames critical inquiry meant to "expose" what has been hidden as distinct from the work of storytelling. The act of exposition, due to procedures driven by suspicion, is destructive in that it seeks to destroy an official narrative. That the destructive critical act may also be an act that restores justice and provides healing for those subjected to the violence of the official narrative is of little consequence to those who profess an allergy to negative critique. (This is not to say that the work of exposition is not worthy in and of itself.) Though she admits that "we need critique; we absolutely need it," Haraway conveys an urgency in the work of addition, rather than exposition, de-sedimentation, and deconstruction. "Our politics these days," she says, "require us to . . . figure out how, with each other, we can open up possibilities for what can still be. And we can't do that in a negative mood" (Weigel 2019).

Haraway celebrates Vinciane Despret's "worlding practice" while describing her as "allergic to denunciation and hungry for discovery, needy for what must be known and built together, with and for earthly beings, living, dead, and yet to come" (Haraway 2016b: 127). Despret's work is driven by "the virtue of politeness," which Haraway connects to Hannah Arendt's notion of "to go visiting," or "the ability to find others actively interesting, even or especially others most people claim to know all too completely" (Haraway 2016b: 127). Undergirded by curiosity, this is a method of "learning and teaching polite inquiry" that "enlarges, even *invents* . . . such that the domain of ways of being and knowing dilates, expands, *adds* both to ontological and epistemological *possibilities*, proposes and enacts what was not there enough" (Haraway 2016b: 127 and 126, emphasis added). Haraway delights in the language of "bumptious women" like Despret and Isabelle Stengers in their book, *Women Who Make a Fuss: The Unfaithful Daughters of Virginia Woolf*, a collection of essays about the role of women in the academy, especially in Western Europe. According to Haraway, *Women Who Make a Fuss* calls for "us" to "dare 'to make' the relay; that is to *create*, to *fabulate*, in order not to despair" (Haraway 2016b: 130, emphasis added). That book states that "Vinciane [Despret] wanted to explore the problem of the difference between animals and men, a problem which mobilizes many academic fields . . . where this is usually disputed in terms of identifying 'the human exception,' with remarkable lack of interest or curiosity with regard to animals" (Stengers and Despret 2014: 84). While studying breeders' relationships with the animals they bred, Despret developed a method of constructing a conversation that would "intrigue" correspondents and thus generate the best data (Stengers and Despret 2014: 83). The innovation was to glean from correspondents themselves what questions investigators asked and how the questions were posed in a collaborative, relational exchange. This sounds like a sound ethnographic method vis-à-vis human–human inter-actions, but how does this proposition of collaborative and relational research as curiosity translate into human–nonhuman situations?

In *When Species Meet*, Haraway elaborates on how this curiosity toward the nonhuman animal might ideally instantiate through the work of bioanthropol-ogist Barbara Smuts, whose dissertation research in the 1970s focused on baboons in Kenya and about whom Haraway had written in *Primate Visions*. According to Haraway, Smuts's curiosity prompts her to "learn to look back [at the animal], as well as to recognize that she was looked at, as a core work-practice for doing her science" (Haraway 2008: 23). Moreover, "to respond was to respect; the practice of 'becoming with' rewove the fibers of the scientist's being" (Haraway 2008: 23). The beginnings of the development of this method were not so auspicious, however. Smuts's initial interest in studying chimpan-zees in Tanzania had been thwarted "after being kidnapped and ransomed in the turbulent nationalist and anticolonial human politics of that area of the world in the mid-1970s" (Haraway 2008: 23). In Haraway's retelling, Smuts therefore shifted her research to baboons in Kenya, and, at first, "the monkeys wanted to get as far away from her threatening self as possible" (Haraway 2008: 23). Smuts persisted, however, by "adjusting what she did – and who she was – according to the baboons' social semiotics directed both to her and to one another" (Haraway 2008: 24). Thus she adapted her more traditional training as a scientist as the one who "could query but not be queried" (Haraway 2008: 24). Once she shifted her behavior to mimic how baboons moved – "the way I walked and sat, the way I held my body, and the way I used my eyes and voice" – the baboons "started giving me very deliberate dirty looks, which made me move away" (Haraway 2008: 24). While to me this would signal the baboons' continued rejection of my presence – their possible anti-relationality – to the persistent, young scientist "it signaled a profound change from being treated like an *object* that elicited a unilateral response (avoidable), to being recognized as a subject with whom they could communicate" (Haraway 2008: 25). This new approach allowed Smuts to fulfill her goal of collecting data about the baboons (Haraway 2008: 25).

Without denying that Smuts's shift in behavior from humanlike to baboon-like could have transformed the baboons' approach to her, and that this change in relationship was amenable to both baboons and scientist, I cannot help but focus on the baboons' clear message from the start: no, leave. The baboons in Kenya communicated their possible anti-relational stance from the outset, which Smuts and Haraway translate as a *lack* of communication. Smuts's curiosity and persistence begat new methods of engagement; even after the recalibration, the baboons' message continued to be no. At some point, it must have become clear to the baboons that the scientist was there to stay. What Haraway extolls as curiosity, a curiosity that births relational "becoming-with," I would call, in this case, disrespect.

What if we consider that Smuts's case entails not only or merely that the scientist had to shift her behavior to accommodate the baboons, but rather, and more pointedly, that the baboons were coerced into accommodating her? Haraway notes that the baboons were "redone too, in baboon ways, by having entangled their gaze with that of this young clipboard-toting human female" (Haraway 2008: 25). The phrasing "entangled their gaze" suggests that the baboons had sought this relation when, in fact, in Haraway's retelling, the baboons had repeatedly communicated rejection. The baboons' communication was translated into an amenable difficulty that had to be overcome until the desired outcome was reached.

How does the other, an other who does not or cannot see the benefit of the exchange, speak their anti-relationality outside of direct violence? Krista Thompson writes about an early twentieth-century postcard that featured a Jamaican woman in a headscarf defiantly staring into the camera lens with the typed caption: "Chuh!!" In handwriting, the postcard sender had added: "Wha for you look 'pon me like dat? You is well forward! Chuh! – Ely" (Thompson 2006: 18). Along with other postcards that Thompson found during her research, this postcard, the woman's pose, and both printed and personalized captions "suggest that some tourists may have heard such remarks on their own photographic excursions" (Thompson 2006: 18). Indeed, Thompson continues, some tourist narratives describe "reluctant inhabitants who variously demanded monetary compensation . . ., engaged in 'staring contests' (and often won) . . ., or physically attacked the photographer (biting the ear of the picture-taker, by one account, literally consuming the tourist devoted to visual consumption)" (Thompson 2006: 18–19). Yet these postcards and captions rendering light-hearted these anti-relational modes of communication nevertheless exist for us to see. That is, the modes of anti-relation were not entirely successful. These postcards translated the colonized and racial other's clear rejection of the terms of relation offered by the tourist – saying, perhaps, "Don't take my picture, tourist / Leave me be, white man," to cite Haitian poet Felix Morisseau-Leroy's "Tourist" – into a photographable event that is translated into charming, local color, perversely abetting that which the other had communicated against. This comparison between primate animal otherness and black(ened) person other-ness is not my own collapse, but rather the collapse evident in various colonial and postcolonial texts.[38]

Contrasted with Smuts's practice of "look[ing] back" at the baboons, in a banal morning encounter with his house cat, Haraway argues that Algerian-French philosopher Jacques Derrida "failed a simple obligation of companion species; he did not become curious about what the cat might actually be doing, feeling, thinking, perhaps making available to him in looking back at him that morning" (Haraway 2008: 20). Writing about the published version of a 1997 lecture called *The Animal That Therefore I Am*, Haraway details her utter disappointment at this "most curious of men, among the most committed and able of philosophers to spot what arrests curiosity" and who "nurtur[es] an entanglement and a *generative* interruption called response" (Haraway 2008: 20, emphasis added). According to Haraway, because Derrida's "own deep interest in animals is coextensive with his practice as a philosopher," she is "shocked" by Derrida's "incuriosity," which led him to "mis[s] a possible invitation, a possible introduction to other-worlding" (Haraway 2008: 20).

Evident in the lecture is Derrida's deconstructive procedure, rather than the positivism Haraway prizes, in relation to what the Western philosophical tradition has called "the animal." Derrida dwells on a concept for a significant length of time in the male Western philosophical genealogy before he subtly but distinctly moves on to the next semiotic "barnacle." One gets the sense that

---

[38] Colin Dayan, for instance, notes that Edward Long's *History of Jamaica* (1774) "draws an analogy between the negro and the orangutan, whose brain is 'mere matter alone,' unanimated with a thinking principle" (Dayan 1998: 194). For more on this association between black(ened) people and beasts and animals, see Jackson 2020.

Derrida finds inadequacy among many of these concepts and approaches and his reading procedure prioritizes de-sedimentation rather than petrification, naming, categorizing, and building. Haraway's interpretation seems to confuse Derrida's keen attention to certain topics – specifically human shame and animal suffering – for espousal. Derrida's focus on his "shame" at being naked in front of his cat, which gazes back at him, an obviously comedic meditation, is not a straightforward admission that shame forecloses reciprocal relationality between cat and human; he deconstructs the long genealogy of thought, including the biblical Adamic tradition, that would have him think so. In another case, Derrida humors for many pages (or minutes) Jeremy Bentham's question of whether the animal suffers, remaining dissatisfied with the language endemic to such a question, but without reaching a resolution. This mode of unsatisfied de-sedimentation differs markedly from Haraway's characterization that Derrida turns to Bentham because "he had nowhere else to go" (Haraway 2008: 22). In fact, Derrida critiques the disturbing confidence in moments in the thinking of philosophers, including Descartes, Kant, Heidegger, and Lacan, when he writes that "males not females, for that difference is not insignificant," who "go on as if they themselves have never been looked at, and especially not naked, by an animal that addressed them" (Derrida 2008: 13–14).

Haraway's usage of Derrida in *When Species Meet* models a rejection of deconstructive critique and an embrace of positivism. Despite her call to decenter the human, this defense of positivism relies on a faith in the human capacity to apprehend everything, including what a cat may be "thinking" as it stares at a naked person. "As a philosopher," Haraway writes, "he [Derrida], knew nothing more *from, about, and with* the cat at the end of the morning than he knew at the beginning, no matter how much better he understood the root scandal as well as the enduring achievements of his textual legacy" (Haraway 2008: 22,). According to Zakiyyah I. Jackson, in this lecture Derrida maintains that the "question of 'the animal' in philosophy refers 'not to the animal but to the naïve assurance of man,'" and, from this perspective, the question becomes "whether what calls itself human has the right rigorously to attribute to man, which means therefore to attribute to himself, what he refuses the animal, and whether he can ever possess the pure, rigorous, indivisible concept, as such, of that attribution" (Jackson 2020: 57). Jackson wonders, then, "what of the capacities that exceed human identification? What of those things and creatures with which is not (yet) possible to confer identification or with which identification and sense making that disqualifies from ethical consideration all those incalculable opacities and yet-to-be-recuperated differences with which it does not and, by design, cannot identify" (Jackson 2020: 57).

Derrida's attentiveness to what cannot be known from a human perspective can be contrasted with Haraway's faith in the ability of (social) scientific methods to shed light on all opacities. To what extent can the biologist, anthropologist, or primatologist perceive beyond "human" capacity? From her own retelling, Smuts's time with the baboons changed her sensorial attunement to her world, but can we describe this becoming-with and becoming-as baboon as proof of her having exceeded her "human" "sense making," or is this another form of "sentimental ethics" that centers the properly considered (white liberal subject) human self's ability to experience as the other without being the other? These and other valences of eco-criticism with animal studies and posthumanism share common ground with nineteenth-century abolitionist sentimentalism and its faith in empathetic relation with an other from a secure, human position.

Derrida's refusal to delve into the extended interspecies conversation with the cat with whom he lives can be described as an acceptance that there is and will always be an "incalculable opacity" and a difference that Derrida not only would not wish to subsume, but in such an attempt, would locate a brutal desire. In Haraway's text, the desire for science-abetted, human-induced communication takes for granted that the cat can and must be made to make itself increasingly transparent to the human. The text insists that "positive knowledge of and with animals might just be possible, knowledge that is positive in quite a radical sense if it is not built on the Great Divides" (Haraway 2008: 21). In this game of safe relationality for the human, does the human become more transparent to the cat? On what terms? In what language? Does the cat "care"? Does it matter to the human whether the cat "cares"? Did it matter to Smuts that the baboons rejected her presence repeatedly before acquiescing to her demands for further communication and "transparency"? To what extent is this valuing of human-led interspecies communication – in which the human claims to know more about the nonhuman at the end of the day, and in which the human cannot, from the human position, presume that the nonhuman harbored this desire – another form of the human-centrism and anthropocentrism that Haraway repeatedly admonishes?

In *A Small Place* (1988), a searing critique of British colonialism and tourism in Antigua, Jamaica Kincaid offers her own take on curiosity and politeness. She writes:

> You came. You took things that were not yours, and you did not even, for appearances' sake, ask first. You could have said, "May I have this, please?" and even though it would have been clear to everybody that a yes or no from us would have been of no consequence you might have looked so much better ... I would have had to admit that at least you were polite ... There must have been some good people among you, but they stayed home. And that is the point. They stayed home. (Kincaid 2000: 34–35)

Kincaid sarcastically mocks the English value of politeness considering the obvious "impoliteness" of British imperialism, based on taking rather than "asking." The implied joke here is that it is absurd to expect the (white) English to have considered the Indigenous people they encountered both in the Americas and Africa worthy of their famed politesse. In Kincaid's long essay, the ethics are clear: to "stay home," incurious, is the relative "good" (Kincaid 2000: 35). This colonized black person's claim to anti-relation renders farcical the pervasive "we" of ecological writings. The consequences of European curiosity includes not knowing "what we were like before we met you." People like the "you" in the book, on the other hand, can see "your" names reflected in the names of streets all over the Caribbean and libraries and schools that "glorif[y]" "your" history and "eras[e] mine" (Kincaid 2000: 36). "Even if I really came from people who were living like monkeys in trees," she concludes, "it was better to be that than what happened to me, what I became after I met you" (Kincaid 2000: 37).[39]

The larger problem I have been describing throughout is not merely interspecies entanglement itself. In the essay cited by Haraway, called "Encounters with Animal Minds," Smuts describes her months with the baboons as she adjusted to their instincts vis-à-vis the weather, prey, and predators, as well as the dog with whom she shared her life back in the United States. Smuts's essay reminded me of Colin Dayan's complex, history-laden accounts of her relationships with various wild and domesticated animals. Dayan's writings in *With Dogs at the End of Life* (2015) and *Animal Quintet* (2020) do not shy away from the violent histories of racialization and poverty interlaced with how people, specifically in relation to the law, live with wild and domesticated animals. Her descriptions of life with various dogs are visceral, emotional, even passionate. What strikes me about both Smuts's and Dayan's writings about their relationships with animals is how little *use* or *utility* shapes the writing.

In contrast, several eco-critics' instrumentalization of human–nonhuman relations reveal their secular Christian, especially Protestant, value system's underpinnings. Even as many of these writings explicitly bemoan the havoc that secularized Christian thought wreaked on parts of the world colonized by Britain – with their misunderstandings of how non-English people used the land and nonhuman animals to sustain them – these writings also contain whispers of a Protestant desire for utility. Though claiming that her Catholic upbringing influenced her materialist approach to the world, I would argue that Haraway's thinking is underpinned by secular Protestantism.[40] This Protestant

---

[39] I do not interpret this as Kincaid's belief in a pure, African "before," but, rather, as a pessimistic statement on so-called humanity in colonialism.

[40] Haraway repeatedly insists on the influence of Catholicism on her thinking, especially in Haraway and Nichols Goodeve 2000: 8–13, 24, 86, 107, 121, and 141.

underpinning surfaces in references as direct as the John Bunyan's *Pilgrim's Progress* (1678), to which she compares her essay "The Promises of Monsters," and more subtly in the sinews of her positivist thinking (Haraway 1991: 295, 301, and 303). The desire to instrumentalize what *is*, to render biological and cultural entanglements into positivist imperatives, strikes me as profoundly Protestant. The danger with this instrumentalization, I insist, is its concomitant reliance on rewriting or erasing history.

Rewriting is itself a crucial component of Haraway's method. She is inspired by what she describes as the "anti-elitist . . . reading conventions" of the science fiction world, which, unlike "academically propagated, respectful consumption protocols," invite "rewriting" (Haraway 1991: 326).[41] To make her case, she turns to John Varley's Nebula award–winning SF story, "Press Enter" (1984), in which the character of Lisa Foo suffers a "superabundantly" violent killing; her "eyes and brain congealed and her breasts [which contain implants] horribly melted" (Haraway 1991: 327). Though admitting that the violence of her death "really is not alright," Haraway's reading strategy is not to critique, reject, or contextualize the story but to instead "rewrite" it (Haraway 1991: 327). She wants to "rearticulate the figure of Lisa Foo to unsettle the closed logics of a deadly racist misogyny" (Haraway 1991: 327). To do so, however, is to deny the fact of the story's existence such as it is. This desire to rewrite this story – or to express and defend the desire to rewrite it – instead of writing an entirely different story or analyze the one that exists, as it exists, is confounding. Haraway persists that to dismiss "Press Enter" as "a conventional heterosexual romance, bourgeois detective fiction, technophobic-technophilic fantasy, dragon-lady story, and, finally, white masculinist narrative" "does serious violence to the subtle tissues of the story's writing" (Haraway 1991: 327). *Really*? Despite Haraway's repeated critiques of white male thinkers, her defense of the misogyny and racism that grounds this part of the story seems to stem from a desire to defend "generativity" at all costs. To be clear, I am not arguing for the story to be censored or destroyed. Rather, I defend the value of critical readings that would analyze the story as it is – not as one would wish it to be. Haraway claims that "the point of differential/oppositional rewriting is not to make the story come out 'right' [but to] rearticulate the figure of Lisa Foo to unsettle the closed logics of a deadly racist misogyny" (Haraway 1991: 327). This reading praxis may be sensible and even welcomed in the SF context from which Haraway culls it, but not every kind of narrative can be manipulated thusly.

---

[41] Haraway also considers science fiction "a political theory" (Haraway and Nichols Goodeve 2000: 120).

Haraway's usage of the term "contact zone" also instantiates what Terrefe might call "writing as revision" (Terrefe 2020: 135). Haraway recalls that she had learned the term "from colonial and postcolonial studies in my political and academic life" (Haraway 2008: 216). A coinage by literary scholar Mary Louise Pratt in her book *Imperial Eyes* (1992), the term "refer[s] to the space of imperial encounters, the space in which peoples geographically and historically separated come into contact with each other and establish ongoing relations, usually involving conditions of coercion, radical inequality, and intractable conflict" (Pratt 2007: 8). This is not the definition that Haraway cites, instead plucking the following description into *When Species Meet*: the term "treats the relations . . . in terms of co-presence, interaction, interlocking understandings and practices, often within radically asymmetrical relations of power" (cited in Haraway 2008: 216). Combined, both quotes more fully define the term as Pratt uses it in her work, but it is revealing that Haraway only cites the section that speaks to the relational entanglements – even if "asymmetrical" – rather than the constitutive violence that forced entanglement in the first place. Haraway then shifts to Jim Clifford's 1997 adaptation of the term by "demonstrat[ing] how 'the new paradigms begin with historical contact, with entanglement at intersecting regional, national, and transnational levels. Contact approaches presuppose not sociocultural wholes subsequently brought into relationship, but rather systems already constituted relationally, entering new relations through historical processes of displacement'" (cited in Haraway 2008: 217). What begins as a term that articulates the complex valences of the violent inequalities of conquest and colonization ends in Haraway's "add[ing] naturalcultural and multispecies matters to Clifford's open net bag" (Haraway 2008: 217). That is, what Pratt structures as a distinctly hierarchical set of relations turns into a rhizomic discussion of "hybridity" and, finally, into interspecies entanglement (Clifford 1999: 7).

Haraway does not actually rewrite "Press Enter," and I wonder about the rhetorical value of calling for "rewriting" as a method without actually doing so. I also wonder what her rewritten version would be. Would Lisa Foo not die at all? Would her death be less violent? "Foo can be a guide through the terrains of virtual space," imagines the text, "but only if the fine lines of tension in the articulated webs that constitute her being remain in play, open to the unexpected reality of an unlikely hope" (Haraway 1991: 327). Foo *can be* a guide in Haraway's imagined rewriting, but she *is not* in the Nebula award–winning story.

4.4 Violence and The Creation of Compost

"The alchemists called the overall process that occurred during the Nigredo as mortification, which meant to them 'facing the dead part.' In the lab, mortification results in a powder or ashes in which the characteristics of the former can no longer be recognized."

Dennis William Hauck, *The Complete Idiot's Guide to Alchemy*[42]

What I call "compost-mania" – Haraway's "we are all compost," Lisa Wells's "to be a field of poppies," and Monique Allewaert's claim of agency for "parahumanity" – elides a long history of uneven incorporation and extraction. The black(ened) position's defining and unchosen state of being becomes an ethics of becoming that always remains rhetorical. (I am not aware of any ecological writer choosing to [die to] become compost.) White ecological desires "to become compost" as a form of becoming-with in the world buries blackness as compost for the white(ned) subject, or, rather, as that which must perish for itself to generate new life-forms. Not only does white humanity/ subjectivity exist in relation to black "humanity"/"subjectivity," but also white humanity/subjectivity relies on black(ened) abjection, fungibility/compostability, and obscured suffering. As Ruha Benjamin argues in her response to Haraway's slogan "Make Kin, Not Babies": "vampirically, white vitality feeds on black demise" (Benjamin 2018: 41).

The violation of black people's bodies becomes the central metaphor in Monique Allewaert's *Ariel's Ecology*. Unlike other ecological writings, Allewaert's literary analysis of various colonial texts from and about the Caribbean and North America engages directly with the history of enslavement and blackness. However, this engagement ends up reinstating blackness as compost through her concept of "parahumanity" and who and what it is useful for.

Allewaert investigates various colonial texts to show, first, that "colonials" (i.e., Europeans and Euro-Americans) were anxious about the "transformation of human and other bodies" in contact with the natural world, especially in what Allewaert calls "the tropics" (Allewaert 2013: 2). Second, she notes that these anxious texts show that these transformations were especially endured by "those persons claimed as property in the colonies, particularly by Afro-American persons" (Allewaert 2013: 2). She defines this transformation in "the tropics" as that which "produced a different materialist tradition in which the body (animal or vegetable) is invaded, rendered in parts, and otherwise deranged" (Allewaert 2013: 3). While "catastrophic" for both whites (worried about tropical corruption of "their vigor and morality") and blacks, "whose destruction by climactic and economic structures was legally justified by metropolitan and colonial law," "it also indicates," to Allewaert, "that the Americas gave rise to an alternative materialism of the body" (Allewaert

---

[42] Hauck 2008: 128.

2013: 3). In other words, the process that "deranges" the black body generates a potentiality for other beings.

Building on eighteenth-century vitalist materialism, which held that "atoms and other invisible particles and fluids … possess agency that is not dependent on their organizations into bodies," Allewaert finds "agency" in what she calls these "missing parts" (Allewaert 2013: 52 and 13). While two chapters of her book explore with complexity how black people re-narrativized a world that sought to violently break them in body and in spirit, Allewaert makes an addition that undermines the very grounds of that part of her argument. She does so through a framing that transforms accounts of relentless violation from the black(ened) position into a framework that can be *generative* for the non-black(ened), or white(ned), position. Defining her term of "parahumanity," Allewaert enumerates that it was "opened up by colonials attempting to manage black persons, particularly their capacity for collective resistance"; what rendered "parahumans" "distinguishable from other bodies produced in emerging biopolitical regimes" is that "her body was broken in parts: an ear amputated for petit marronage, a hand for theft, an arm pulled from the body by the sugar mill, and sometimes a head cut from the body for resistance so total as to warrant death" (Allewaert 2013: 85). Despite this quite specific definition that could echo how I and others define the black(ened) position, for Allewaert, "parahumanity" as a term is itself necessary for her logic to proceed, for it usefully "gave rise to a minoritarian mythos of the Americas in which the autonomy of parts engenders new musings" (Allewaert 2013: 102 and 25). That is, "parahumanity" as a supposed state of being defined by black mutilation can be a source of inspiration rather than fear for those whose state of being is not mutilatably black.

Allewaert argues that, to eighteenth-century thinkers, *everyone* had the potential to slip into parahumanity, and the rise of trans-Atlantic slavery and colonialism in the Americas provided a convenient route to project outward this terror of the potential inner parahuman (Allewaert 2013: 102). Rather than think through the notion of parahumanity as a violently imposed state of (non)being, in which the human imposes parahumanity onto a certain population and its subsequent generations, Allewaert shifts attention to her parahumans' *agentic* religious, material, and discursive negotiations with death for generalizable meaning. For instance, Allewaert "propose[s] that tracing the figure of the parahuman in the eighteenth and nineteenth centuries reveals a perversion of the category of the human that was effected by diasporic Africans' *performance* of their parahumanity" (Allewaert 2013: 86, emphasis added). To describe these negotiations as a "performance" suggests that parahumanity was defined by what the parahuman *willed* rather than what was *forced onto* the parahuman.

That is, there arises an equivalence between parahumans' varied responses and negotiations (e.g., the "creole stories" and "fetishes" Allewaert discusses) and the imposed condition of their state of being (e.g., the literal breaking of the blackened body into parts, which Allewaert also discusses).

Allewaert's set of arguments, which at times contradict each other, might be difficult to follow. Nevertheless, I try to outline the book's logic thusly: (1) the parahuman was forcibly created by torture and mutilation or the rendering into parts; (2) the parahuman labors, lives, and makes culture within this *de jure* and *de facto* state of things; (3) finally, in the signature eco-critical and vitalist spin, both the coerced "openness" of parahumanity and the narratives and other technologies that stem from a need to heal, soothe, protect, and prevent further destruction of the parahuman body and spirit provide possibilities for "new" ways of being for those in the position defined by the power to generate parahumanity by having the legal and customary space to break apart the black(ened) body. The text describes these possibilities: "Parahumanity is not, then, a suspension of the category of the human that involves not-choosing. It is a parasitism and a paradox in which choosing keeps the nonchosen in play as a potentiality" (Allewaert 2013: 111). According to the text, parahumanity is a state of *becoming-with* for *everyone* in its perpetual "potentiality" that prioritizes addition and dynamism, even though this additive and dynamic state and way of being relies on subtraction and fixity for the black(ened) entity.

The book's contention that parahumans are not hierarchically below humans or above animals, but that all exist on the same plane, is crucial, for this logic, such as it is, on which the book relies falls apart with any acknowledgment of hierarchy (Allewaert 2013: 110). The book further attempts to distance the argument from considerations of antagonism and verticality – that is, one group's existence as reliant on the destruction and suffering of the other – when she insists that the parahuman, while not "prior" to or below the human, is "parasitic on and thus after and also beside the human" (Allewaert 2013: 110). The text claims that the parahuman can "choose" to adopt human traits as well as other traits, rendering it (the parahuman) parasitic. Suddenly, the parahuman, as parasitic on humanity, is defined not by forced subjugation, but instead by an enviable and performance-based dynamism. This definition of the parahuman that centers the parahuman's will and choice (to take part in the human) contradicts entirely the book's first definition of the parahuman, which is a state imposed by humans and on which humans *parasitically* rely on, as the book itself acknowledges, to maintain the façade of humanity (Allewaert 2013: 110).

David Marriott's *On Black Men* explores how white desire for and hatred of blackness instantiates in the most horrific forms of violence through a focus on lynching and lynching photography Robert Mapplethorpe's photographs of black men and critics' reactions to them; and Jeffrey Dahmer's murders of black and Asian men, his photographs of their carefully rearranged body parts, and his subsequent cannibal consumption of them. Regarding Dahmer's composed photographs, Marriot writes that they "ma[p] bodies naked and abed, ripped open and dismembered, innards exposed, eyes staring out at the camera from decapitated heads" (Marriott 2000: 34). After the dismembering, both the photographic commemoration and the cannibalization evinced Dahmer's "desire to see and to devour" and "to make them a 'permanent part of [him]" (Marriott 2000: 35). Dahmer's racialized consumption of black(ened) people made flesh is a form of composting, becoming-with, and addition-as-subtraction indistinguishable from the kinds of additions discussed in Allewaert's readings of the mutilated "parahuman" being compost for the becoming-with of the one transformed by this generative destruction. In Marriott's reading, the metaphor of burial repeatedly emerges in relation to Dahmer's desire to ingest these black(ened) men's corpses and to transform them into another kind of life, *for* Dahmer. "Buried deep inside him," writes Marriott, "*– dead but breathing, living because dead –* his victims were kept secret, deposited, to be *swallowed and exhumed* again and again" (Marriott 2000: 38–39, emphasis added).

Writing about the 1685 *Code noir*, Colin Dayan states that "in the specific kind of reduction and evisceration of humans outlined [in this document], nothing, not even 'kindness,' can alleviate the slave's condition. This is the terror" (Dayan 1998: 206). This terror and the impossibility of redress in the face of "reduction," and relentless subtraction, is then transformed in *Ariel's Ecology* into potentiality. Consider this scene of torture cited by Dayan, in which Père Jean-Baptiste Labat, a missionary in the service of Louis XIV, describes his punishment of an enslaved black man who had tried to heal another slave by using "an idol":

> I tied up the sorcerer, and I dealt out around three hundred lashes of the whip that flayed him from the shoulders to the knees. He cried out in despair, and our negroes asked me to have mercy on him, but I told them that sorcerers did not feel pain, and that he cried in order to mock me. (Dayan 1998: 206)

After this flaying was done, he proceeded to "was[h] him with a pimentade, 'a pickling brine in which you crush red pepper and citrons,'" and which "caused 'a horrible pain ... but [was] a certain cure for gangrene'" (Dayan 1998: 206). Dayan describes this set of acts thusly: "You harm, and then you alleviate the harm you have caused." In so doing, "the executioner also gets to be the savior; the benevolence continues the brutalization, while claiming otherwise" (Dayan

2008: 206). Further, the prolongation of the torture also protects the property. In Saint-Domingue, this was a quotidian scene of how enslaved blacks were made into "parahumans" – the mutilations and forms of breaking and forcing the body into an unasked-for porosity – that Allewaert's book considers with optimism. Who benefits from the "potentiality" and "generativity" issuing from this set of acts becomes clear, and it is certainly not the "parahuman." Punishment and torture of the black-(ened) body yield "benevolence" and other positive affects and attributes for the white(ned) subject.

It is not at all farfetched to consider what Allewaert writes about alongside Marriott's and Dayan's descriptions of the "gratuitous" violence, to borrow Wilderson's term, of dismemberment (Wilderson 2010: 17 and 55). It may seem strange to transform these tortures into generative becoming-with, but this is the procedure in *Ariel's Ecology* and other ecological and vitalist writings.[43] Unlike *Ariel's Ecology* and other vitalist and ecological writings, Dayan's and Marriott's discussions do not productively transform the destruction of the black person into a universalized, multispecies "we."

Citing Isabelle Stengers on her concept of symbiosis, Allewaert, like Haraway, admits that "the relation among parts ... is not harmonious," which means that "when a symbiosis or compromise is formed it always excludes and even *violates* some of the entities that compose it and that might resist it" (Allewaert 2013: 70, emphasis added). Moreover, "despite the terror this openness evokes," "this process of mediation can strengthen, weaken, or eliminate that body, but in all cases it continually transforms and diversifies the body" (Allewaert 2013: 19). Although the "bodies" most susceptible to the "terror" of "openness," including the "weakening" and "elimination" rather than "strengthening," are black(ened) people's bodies, Allewaert asserts that "what Orlando Patterson has called spaces of social death ... was a condition that touched not just Afro-Americans but *all persons* moving through the colonies" (Allewaert 2013: 25, emphasis added). In what turns out to be a fantasy or speculative fabulation of the past, not only is the terror of forced relationality meted out evenly across "all persons" in the colonial Americas, but also these "cultures of social death were not simply sites of tragedy and loss" (Allewaert 2013: 25). The text continues, "bodies and persons pulled part, trespassed, and brutalized in these regions produced modes of story [parahuman

---

[43] Some black ecological writings follow a procedure that ends up in the same place. In that case, the black thinker rhetorically transforms a historical circumstance of black suffering and renders it "generative," in some way, for everyone's futurity.

tales], artifactual creation [fetishes], and fantasy [of decomposing and recomposing bodies]" (Allewaert 2013: 25).

I will briefly outline how the white person is transformed by proximity to parahumanity through Allewaert's interpretation of Leonora Sansay's *Secret History; or, the Horrors of St. Domingo, in a Series of Letters Written by a Lady at Cape Francois to Col. Burr, Late Vice-President of the United States, Principally during the Command of General Rochambeau* (1808) and *Zelica* (1820). *Secret History* is an epistolary text that recounts the last days of the Haitian Revolution from the perspective of a white Philadelphian wife. Though it evinces the expected, anti-black, pro-planter allegiances, Allewaert "read[s] Sansay's text against its own desires" (Allewaert 2013: 149). First, she adopts Joseph Roach's concept of surrogation to explain how Sansay portrays "white women who gain autonomy by repeating Afro-American performances of politics and personhood" (Allewaert 2013: 148). Second, rather than collapse difference entirely, Allewaert argues, the white performer's surrogation reestablishes racial difference and white supremacy "not simply [as] a process of recollection and displacement but also [as] one of addition" (Allewaert 2013: 148 and 159). My critique stems mostly from the instrumentalization that Allewaert's interpretive process shares with other eco-critiques – in this case, the transformation of surrogacy-as-addition into an ethics of becoming.[44]

Many counterrevolutionary portrayals of the Haitian Revolution focused on "the destruction and violation of white women's bodies," which, according to Allewaert, "suggests that what was at stake was not only a shifting of political symbolics but a destruction of the modes of genealogy and family associated with and founded on the careful management of (white) women's bodies" (Allewaert 2013: 162). *Ariel's Ecology* argues that, in this derangement of the white woman's body, a derangement that had theretofore been structurally and systemically enacted onto and against black(ened) people's bodies in the colonies, is an opening to an addition that shifts the terms of white personhood, even in death.

Writing about Sansay's novel *Zelica*, which has similar themes to *Secret History*, Allewaert focuses on the mourning ablutions performed on the corpse of Clara, the white protagonist, by a Vodou priestess. Through this ritual, Allewaert argues that "she is changing from a closed to an opened body, from a racially determined 'white' identity that nonetheless mimics Afro-American

---

[44] Allewaert's discussion also excludes mention of how "Sansay dwells on white ladies' rage and infidelities rather than the pain and suffering of their socially subordinate rivals" (Dayan 1998: 181). That is, though it is relevant to her discussion about white womanhood, Allewaert's interpretation expunges white women's complicity in the violent system that was being toppled.

practices to a creole and Haitian person" (Allewaert 2013: 169) According to this interpretation, Sansay's writings not only evince surrogation – mimesis, replacement, and differentiation – but also *becoming* "place" (Haiti), if only after death. "*Zelica* traces ... a becoming Haitian," proposes Allewaert, "in which women's autonomy was not predicated on their relations to men and was not in any simple way equivalent to death" (Allewaert 2013: 153). In death, Clara's body undergoes a process meant to restore the tortured black body. "For all its negativity," Allewaert writes,

> Sansay's work strives to instantiate a *productivity*. The surrogation through which Sansay attempts to negotiate this shift is, *however racially problem-atic*, an operation that allows an opening to the movements of counternorma-tive desires, agencies, and socialities ... Yet even if Sansay's productivity remains only a trajectory, it opens the critical project of following the curve of her involution to defamiliarize and pluralize our understandings of agency in the period so that they attend to the impact and dissemination of Afro-American modes of personhood and resistance. (Allewaert 2013: 171, emphasis added)

Allewaert's argument that the white heroine becomes a new kind of Haitian subject relies on her receiving the Vodou rites of mourning, some of which are meant to help the spirit "joi[n] the ancestors under the waters in the mythical place called *Ginen* (Guinea)" (Dayan 1998: 261). The fantasy of becoming that *Ariel's Ecology* reads into the text assumes a Haiti that is necessarily "available" *to them* – Clara and Sansay – despite Haiti's founding as a nation of blacks who revolted against slavery and white supremacy (Allewaert 2013: 172). In this fantasy, Clara's subjectivity, as well as the blacks' responsibility and obeisance to her, never ends, even with her death; even Vodou, a system and technology that responds to the violence of colonialism, is available to and for her becoming.[45] The Vodou priestess's talents and skills ensure that the white heroine can also occupy the space of this multiracial afterlife. What Allewaert reads against the grain of the text and earlier interpretations of the novel as a productive reevaluation of "agency" in the colonies, I interpret, rather, as a desire in the novel "to colonize the afterlife" (Benjamin 2018: 42). The addition that Allewaert reads in *Zelica* is mined from the subtractions that transformed African persons into parahumans.

Ariel's Ecology maintains that interspecies relationality and an openness to the world outside one's body (a body one may not actually "possess" by law) provides an antidote to staid European and Euro-American individualism. Of

---

[45] Both Dayan and Rachel Beauvoir-Dominique suggest that Vodou is best understood in relation to colonialism and slavery rather than in the intellectual and spiritual tradition of African continuity (Dayan 1998 and Beauvoir-Dominique 1995).

this kind of optimism, Achille Mbembe writes: "From the standpoint of the conqueror, the colony is a world of limitless subjectivity" (Mbembe 2001: 189). This optimism is echoed in the summary of *Ariel's Ecology*'s back cover, which soothes (itself): "The transformation of colonial subjectivity into ecological personhood is not a nightmare; rather, it is a mode of existence that was, until now, only glimmering in Che Guevara's dictum that postcolonial resistance is synonymous with 'perfect knowledge on the ground.'" At the core of this message is the desire to assuage white anxiety that the human body is not actually an enclosed, independent entity, rather than to seriously consider black anxieties about the fact of forced, violent porosity.

4.5 From the Soil Grows the White *Indigène*

"Are you waste or compost?" asks the main page of the website for Loop Living Cocoon, a company that makes coffins from mycelium. "Mycelium," continues the ad copy, "is nature's biggest recycler. What if we collaborate with nature to enrich life after death?" Invented by Dutch biodesigner Bob Hendrikx, the coffin allows "people to become one with nature again. We can enrich the soil instead of polluting it" (Henley 2020). Visitors to the Living Cocoon's website learn about why choosing a "living coffin" might be the best use of one's corpse. Instead of uselessly decomposing in a wooden coffin, for which a tree had to be sacrificed, it could "increas[e] biodiversity," be "biodegradable," and help "new nature grow" through its composition grown from mycelium, "the underground fungal network of mushrooms." Shortening the common process of decomposition in a traditional coffin, the Living Cocoon allows the corpse to become nutritious for the soil within "two to three years" (Henley 2020).

On the second episode of the television series *Hannibal*, clairvoyant FBI agent Will Graham (Hugh Dancy) helps track a mycelium-obsessed serial killer (Aidan Devine) who buries his victims alive to grow mushrooms. Burying his diabetic victims in a "high nutrient compost" and feeding them sugar intravenously "long enough for the circulatory systems to . . . feed the mushrooms," the killer fulfilled his fantasy of hyper-relationality. Once caught, he tells Graham: "If you walk through a field of mycelium, they know you are there. They know you are there. The spores reach for you as you walk by."

It is not so much that Hendrikx's invention is analogous to the actions of a relation-hungry serial killer, but, rather, that juxtaposing these two fungal scenes denotes how easily the syntax of sustainable compost-mania and vitalism segues into the horror of forced relationality. As Karera notes is the case in Anthropocene writings, a key term throughout *Staying with the Trouble*, as well as other texts of compost-mania and mycelium-delirium, is "relation."[46] Generativity issues from relationality in that relation's import is to generate more life, even if an entity must be destroyed in the process. "We are nutrients, not waste," advertises Hendrikx, which echoes Haraway's repetition of the phrase "We are compost, not posthuman" throughout *Staying with the Trouble*. Though both invoke the first-person plural, these phrases claim to decenter anthropocentrism by reminding us of our bodies' biochemical bottom line.

Though the Living Cocoon enterprise waits for our inevitable death and the serial killer cruelly brings it about, the discourses buttressing both mushroom-friendly environments are curiously similar. In her celebratory account of Recompose, a Washington State-based company that processes human corpses into compost, nonfiction writer and poet Lisa Wells admits to her childhood fantasy of being given a Viking chief's burial, despite the torture that, in some cases, a female slave had to endure by being stabbed and strangled before accompanying her master in the afterlife (Wells 2021b: 39). As in her book *Believers*, Wells shares with the reader a vivid fantasy life in her attempts to narrate herself into a more rooted position in North America while continuously falling back onto the tropes of settler colonialism in the form of the pioneer. She "wanted to live like the kids in the movie; kids who build bonfires, shoot bows and arrows, and defy the authorities. In other words, thinking about the kind of death I wanted taught me about the kind of life I wanted" (Wells 2021b: 38). She wanted the dramatic and poetic burial of a Viking lord, associating her subjectivity with his and not, say, that of his slave.

Published over a year after her book *Believers*, this essay – "To Be a Field of Poppies" – seems to provide the answer to what I will show is the main concern in *Believers*: how can a white person in the United States become "rooted" to the land that Europeans had stolen or acquired under dubious circumstances? A personal and journalistic exploration of communities focused on mitigating the damages barreling us toward the "end of the world," *Believers* is driven by white guilt and the desire for absolution. Though every case study in Wells's book demonstrates a facet of these driving forces, perhaps none exemplifies them more than her discussion of Finisia Medrano.

Medrano, a white transgender woman living "off the grid" in the US Northwest, opens the book. "This book," writes Wells, "began in a place called Sparta, a rugged swath of sparsely populated country near the Oregon–Idaho

---

[46] I succumbed to my own mycelium-delirium by entitling an article, "Mushrooms and Mischief: On Questions of Blackness" (Ramírez-D'Oleo 2019b). Written during an era in which I was still seduced by ecological writings, the essay expresses some ideas with which I would currently disagree.

border. There I spent several days in the temporary encampment of a group of nomadic gardeners, led by a woman named Finisia Medrano" (Wells 2021a: 3). Wells describes Medrano as an "outlaw," whose practices include "trespassing her way through private and public lands, planting wildflowers with edible roots, and attracting the ire of the keepers of order" (Wells 2021a: 3). As Wells and Medrano both admit, "not everyone can get away with – and by that I mean survive – illegally planting on private land" (Wells 2021a: 41). In Medrano's estimations, her actions, from trespassing to making demands on cops, were meant to test "if the white whores of Babylon would murder their own children as readily" (Wells 2021a: 41). Medrano's and her followers' whiteness emerges as a crucial if under-discussed node. Although Medrano and Wells admit that not everyone can "survive" doing the illegal activities Medrano and her follow-ers daily perform, the admission does not shift a fundamental understanding of what this access to free movement in the United States might mean. Medrano's trespassing can be juxtaposed with the arrest or murder of black(ened) people doing nothing illegal, at any time, even in their own homes. "I'm surprised I'm not dead yet," Medrano tells Wells, and Wells responds, "Me too" (Wells 2021a: 43). If both Medrano and Wells admit that whiteness protects Medrano, why is her aliveness and freedom a surprise?

Wells acknowledges that "the stuff [Medrano] said was pointlessly offensive and, at times, blatantly appropriative of Native cultures" (Wells 2021a: 45). Nevertheless, Wells continuously gives her the benefit of the doubt, evinced by the reticence to recount the things Finisia had done that "were 'not so good'" or by claiming that she "couldn't tell if Finisia always meant what she said" (Wells 2021a: 46). Whatever critiques may fall on Medrano in the book are rendered relatively insignificant considering her centrality to the book as a whole; Wells both opens and closes with Medrano as an example of a "believer." Medrano's structural importance in the book suggests that, for Wells, Medrano has "hacked" the problem of becoming rooted as a white person in the United States.

Wells's personal journey to physical and emotional healing become insepar-able from an unbearable guilt and desire to feel rooted. Wells makes this desire explicit in her adoption of French philosopher Simone Weil's definition of rootedness:

> "A human being has roots," writes Simone Weil, "by virtue of his real, active and natural participation in the life of a community which preserves in living shape certain particular treasures of the past and certain particular expect-ations for the future." By this definition, the radical disciples [discussed in the book] were on the path to *becoming rooted.* They believed elements of their inherited version of Christianity were toxic, but rather than reject and dispose

of their faith, or steal someone else's tradition, they told a different version in the spirit of rehabilitation. (Wells 2021a: 100, emphasis added)

Wells's focus on various Christian communities grappling with environmental destruction stems from her search for wisdom while avoiding the cultural vampirism and extraction inherent to various forms of what Philip Deloria calls "playing Indian" (Deloria 1998). Despite these attempts, Wells seems unable to avoid figures like Medrano, who does "play Indian," and who states in a short documentary project about her life: "I'm not Indian. I'm a mad Irishman and an Indian nightmare" (*The Life of Fin* 2018). People like Medrano, who are white and "play Indian," in some way remain attractive to "those, like [Wells], who are effectively rootless" and cannot "fathom what rootedness means, or how it might feel to have roots five hundred generations deep, and to maintain those roots in spite of continuous incursion by an occupying force" (Wells 2021a: 118).

A partially buried but discernible desire found in white-authored eco-logical discourses is to overcome the deep tug of the vastly unequal histor-ical legacies of colonialism and slavery – experienced and dealt with as an individualized spiritual and emotional journey, even when also perfunctorily acknowledged as a set of structural issues – after which one can access rootedness in the so-called New World. Whether it is Medrano's irreverent revamping of Christianity, Haraway's Carrollinian neologisms, or Allewaert's "parahuman" revaluation of black dismemberment, semiotics become a tool of costuming settler colonialist tropes and affects into radical becoming-with.

Recompose, the composting company, literalizes this desire to be "rooted" by becoming part of a soil that would then transform the living (whitened) person's parasitic relationship to the planet into one that, finally, gives back. Far from being a suicidal fantasy, however, Wells's understanding is that Recompose can help her and others attain a kind of immortality. As she repeats throughout, meditating on her own death, for her, becomes a portal into meditating on her life. Although to ponder life's inevitable end is a somewhat banal and accept-able exercise in appreciating the preciousness of life, the language of subjectiv-ity continues even in the fantasy of Wells's material afterlife as compost. "But to leave behind a net-positive legacy," she writes, "to grow something beautiful in death, would be a dream. As a series of attractive promotional cards printed on recycled stock informs me: 'I could be a pinecone,' 'I could be a forest grove,' 'I could be a field of poppies'" (Wells 2021b: 39). Recompose's invitation to potential customers to imagine "being a forest grove" or a "pinecone" begs the question of the metaphysics at play here. Who is this "I" in the fantasy? Though

I cannot verify, there is a likelihood that whatever nonmaterial remains after death – life force, soul, spirit, ghost – is not compostable and will not be the same "I." The "I" here therefore must be the material body, the fruitfully decaying vessel or carapace. The ad copy does not state "my body could be a field of poppies." Why not? Why does the subjectivity of the customer relentlessly remain to maintain the macabre romance? Claire Colebrook might provide an answer to these questions when she writes that the "'we' that is being saved" in these Anthropocene writings is the "'we' that is constituted precisely by way of a death sentence: I mourn my future non-being and therefore I am. Further, I mourn my future non-being and therefore I must do all I can to survive" (Colebrook 2016: 82). As Karera astutely discerns from Colebrook's passage, this "we" is constituted also by a "redemptive nature" (Karera 2019: 38).

The desire to turn one's corpse into something helpful for those who and that which remain alive is, from one point of view, commendable, helpful. Ethically crucial, however, is the question of choice and will; no one can argue that the appropriation of a corpse without the person's consent is anything close to ethical. Yet this is where the history of black people's bodies and corpses enters the frame or was there all along for there to be a frame. Historically, black people have not had the choice in what happens to their bodies. As Ren Ellis Neyra puts it in their critique of José Esteban Muñoz's concept of "brownness" and, more generally, white Latinx people's own alchemical procedure whereby white and *mestizo* (i.e. white(ned) Latin Americans), and their forms of extraction, become "brown" and positively "relational": "Black thought, black culture, and black intramural relation are not ethically bound anywhere on this earth to save anyone nonblack nor to extend an enchantingly reworlding or future-naturalizing hand to any proto-col of nonblack thought" (Ellis Neyra 2020). As Ellis Neyra demonstrates, while blackness may not be "ethically bound" to "save anyone," it remains forced to do so. Even within the ennobling discourse of composting, echoes remain of what Ruha Benjamin sees as white people's potentiality for resurrection: "White people are not just born once, but over and over again, resurrected through law and custom, in order that they kill with impunity" (Benjamin 2018: 41). Indeed, continues Benjamin, "To be white is to colonize the afterlife" (Benjamin 2018: 42). To what extent are the semiotics of composting that sublimate histories of anti-blackness and the afterlives of slavery consonant with attempts to colonize the afterlife? A way to plant a flag not so much on the futurity of homo sapiens, writ large, but on white(ned) life as abetted by innovative claims to non-European lands masquerading as an ecological ethics?

In an endnote that recalls a conversation about the Anthropocene between Haraway and other scholars, Haraway writes that the group "collectively generated the name Plantationocene for the devastating transformation of diverse kinds of human-tended farms, pastures, and forests into extractive and enclosed plantations, relying on slave labor and other forms of exploited, alienated, and usually spatially transported labor" (Haraway 2016b: 206n5).[47] Haraway adds that "the slave plantation system was the model and motor for the carbon-greedy machine-based factory system that is often cited as an inflection point for the Anthropocene" (Haraway 2016b: 206n5). The note then turns to the rhetorical figure of "slave gardens," which "not only provided human food, but also refuges for biodiverse plants, animals, fungi, and soils" (Haraway 2016b: n5). Finally, it claims that "slave gardens are an unexplored world, especially compared to imperial botanical gardens, for the travel and propagation of myriad critters" (Haraway 2016b: 206n5). The claim that "slave gardens" are "unexplored" overlooks scholarship on slavery, the plantation system, Caribbean studies, and black history, as well as the narratives of enslaved and formerly enslaved people and their descendants.

Not only does Haraway's conceptualization of the Plantationocene leave unacknowledged the considerable work done by black writers and scholars writing about the Caribbean, but her elaborations on the term repeatedly distance it from the enslavement of Africans and Afro-descended people. Asked in an interview to elaborate on what she means by the plantation, Haraway responds: "The plantation really depends on very intense forms of labor slavery, including also machine labor slavery, a building of machines for exploitation and extraction of earthlings. I think it is also important to include the forced labor of nonhumans – plants, animals, and microbes – in our thinking" (Mittman 2019).

In another part of the interview, she elaborates on how Central American migrant labor in Texas and California exemplifies what she means by the plantation and the Plantationocene, clarifying that "it's not slavery, but it is the kind of labor force that I associate with plantation conditions" (Mittman 2019). Haraway's repeated attempt to distance the signifier of plantation from associations with blackness, black people, Africa, the Caribbean, and chattel slavery is noteworthy.[48] When, in another interview, she is asked about the role of California in her life and work, Haraway states that "is not about black and white but also made up of an intensely complex history in

---

[47] In the conversation, Noburu Ishikawa defined the plantation as "the slavery of plants." Anna Tsing vocalizes agreement and Haraway adds: "And microbes" (Haraway et al., 2015: 556–557).

[48] In the same interview, Anna Tsing tries to insert signifiers of blackness into the conversation and to give credit to scholars of the Caribbean plantation, seemingly to no avail.

relation to Asia, South America, and Mexico" (Haraway and Nichols Goodeve 2000: 42). She goes on to compare Hortense Spillers and Angela Davis as black women in relation to the signifier of California. The first, in an anecdote that Haraway shares, was considering a position at UC Santa Cruz and "commented on how strange the racial politics out here [in California] felt to her." "Her reference points," Haraway continues, "which were all black and white, were destabilized." Compared to her representation of an anecdotal Spillers, "Davis is a California figure for these last thirty years," having studied under Herbert Marcuse at UC San Diego, been "in prison under Governor Reagan," and "now teaches with us in the History of Consciousness Program. She is a California product as well as a product of the U.S. South" (Haraway and Nichols Goodeve 2000: 42–43). (Full disclosure: I also studied at UC San Diego and lived in California for seven years, but, despite the signifier of *latinidad* that can be applied to me, according to these standards, my Caribbean upbringing likely disqualifies me as a "California product.") I cite these comments at length because several components are striking. The first is that two black women scholars come to stand in for what she and her interviewer call the "black and white" way of thinking race relations in the United States. It is unclear why two white scholars could not come to mind as examples. Blackness and whiteness in this cited "black and white" racial binary are not structural positions but, rather, cultural placeholders like "Mexican" and "Central American." To thus re-narrate the story of layered settler colonialisms – a story that includes Afro-Californios, Afro-Central Americans, and Afro-Mexicans – does not so much complicate the supposed binary, as claimed, but undermines the relevance of blackness to the creation of whiteness – on theological, spatial, as well as epidermal racial scales – and the relationship between whiteness and non-black ethnic categories.[49] This undermining of blackness becomes particularly evident with the anecdote about Spillers and the touting of Davis as having successfully overcome the "black and white" binary seemingly only relevant for blacks in the U.S. South.

At the same time, the mentorship of various Indigenous communities of the Americas is expected to guide "us" out of environmental destruction. This longing for Indigenous guidance in ecological writings emerges alongside their rejection of "modernity," while separating indigeneity from the dynamism of change and adjustment across time. Modernity here signals capitalism, rootlessness or bad (invasive) rooting, the plantation, slave and then wage

---

[49] Pío de Jesus Pico, the last Californio governor happened to be Afro-Mexican. See also Forbes 2010.

labor, and alienation from nature (Haraway 2016b: 157 and Mitman 2019, 4, 12, and 18). The association between blackness – that which was extracted out of various African indigeneities to become a non-Indigenous, non-property-holding, and non-self-possessing entity – and modernity becomes part of the "unthought known" in these ecological writings. If modernity must be rejected in the speculatively fabulated new world of white and (non-black) Indigenous people, then so too must black people, who in the Americas were born out of modernity itself. In eco-criticism, the intolerable stain of modernity tarnishes blackness. In this schematic, blackness is akin to an invasive plant species that cannot ever be properly and generatively rooted *for itself* in the Americas without its contaminating modernity.[50]

In *Staying with the Trouble*, the (non-African) Indigenous elements that can be enlisted into whiteness to form a new (white) indigeneity run the gamut from Navajo string figure practices to the Pima cthulhu spider native to the Western United States.[51] In spite of the spider's scientific name, Haraway wants to "mak[e] a small change . . . from cthulhu to chthulu" so that the spider now connects more closely to the chthonic and distances it and Haraway from Lovecraft's "misogynistic racial-nightmare monster Cthulhu (note spelling difference)" (Haraway 2016b: 101). According to Cecilio Cooper, Haraway's explanation of her half-neologism "intentionally shies away from interpretations of the chthonic associated with American horror writer H. P. Lovecraft" in a move that "seems motivated by a desire to disavow the anti-blackness at the heart of the concept's circulation" (Cooper 2022). What Cooper terms a "pro-indigenous" and "anti-black" "speculative future" "camouflage[d]" by this "anti-Lovecraft posture" necessarily must include white "ongoingness" in the form of joining the always-imagined-as-welcoming, patient, and pedagogically inclined (non-African) Indigenous communities (Cooper 2022).

When black people surface in Wells's writing, they are shrouded in other forms of erasure and absenting. By my count, references to blackness, black people, or black culture number three in *Believers*: a mention of the Black Panther Party, a mention of the League of Revolutionary Black Workers in a listing that also includes "socialist organizations of the 1970s and 1980s" and "twenty-first century anarcho-primitivists," and reference to a tracker who refined his skills helping the Portuguese army maintain colonial strongholds in Angola (Wells 2021a: 180, 144, and 161). None of these references are discussed beyond cursory mention. In contrast, *Believers* carefully notes that many of the intentional communities Wells spends time with include white American or European members with some

---

[50] Modernity here is understood in relation to the re-arrangement of the Western world after 1492, and not in the more colloquial sense of progress or innovation.

[51] For string figures, see Haraway 2016b: 13–14; for spiders, see Haraway 2016b: 31.

exceptions that include members of various Native American nations and "Hispanics" in New Mexico (Wells 2021a: 39, 231, 200, 212, and 220).

This resounding absence of blackness and/or black people is even more stark when we realize that it is not that Wells never encountered black people, or blackness, during her research, but that they were actively absented in at least two crucial ways. The first instance of Wells's sublimation of black people happens when she recounts her short time with The Simple Way, an organization based in Allegheny, an overwhelmingly black neighborhood of North Philadelphia. (According to the 2010 census, the neighborhood was more than 97 percent African American.) Wells describes the group as "multiracial" and only notes race when a white man disrupts the narrative at one point, suggesting that the others in her midst are not white. She also does not describe them as Latinx/Hispanic, though she does in the portions of the chapter set in New Mexico (e.g., "Hispanic, Anglo, and Puebloan residents") (Wells 2021a: 200). The only people lacking in racial or ethnic signifiers seem to be black, but this black presence – which I cannot verify – emerges through absence and through the evocative signifier of Allegheny. The Simple Way's website reveals that it is indeed a multiracial organization, and many of those featured in its images seem to be black, which is not surprising given the demographics of the neighborhood.[52]

The second instance of the absenting of blackness materializes when Wells transforms black poet Harmony Holiday's words about Sun Ra's significance to black culture into a speculative future that can include Wells (Holiday 2019). Holiday's essay speaks of an essence and a black spirit through orality that is in many ways opposed to the impetus of this essay since it gets close to essentialist ideas of a *volk*. Of relevance here is that the world it conjures through Sun Ra's aesthetic imaginary is *specifically for black people*. She writes that Sun Ra's "incantatory poems and musics … tempt us to sing ourselves to the edge of the evil dream that the West has been for Black inhabitants." Wells transforms this black "us" into a misquoted "we" that includes her:

> Those who are ready to "overthrow the West's dead ideas and the habits they demand" make pilgrimage to a territory that is "*after the end of the world* where our sense of sound becomes invincible and whole and grammar is world building and elemental." In this story, after the end of the world there is wholeness, a grammar of "Thou" from which to build the next world. (Wells 2021a: 130)

---

[52] During this visit, Wells has what could be described as a psychic break, which is beyond the scope of this Element to explore, but recalls Toni Morrison's opening example in *Playing in the Dark*.

Wells surreptitiously tucks herself into Holiday's and Sun Ra's fabulations of a world that would not rely on black suffering and extraction. Through this broadened "we," Wells duplicates the extractive relation that Holiday describes thusly: "Black people liv[e] in a *romance* language that is always stealing something from us" (Holiday 2019). Thus Wells miscites an essay that critiques the semiotic malfeasance on which so much of eco-criticism relies. Is this form of "rewriting" also "speculative fabulation"?

5 Recoil and the Speculative

"[B]lack suffering – especially in the figure of slain black bodies – indefinitely haunts the possibility of a post-apocalyptic political afterlife. What 'black death' promises, instead, is a post-apocalyptic world without any signs of ethical transformation."

   Axelle Karera, "Blackness and the Pitfalls of Anthropocene Ethics"[53]

"Black life is replaced by more black life over the generations. It never dies. It is only replaced in the next generation; and because it is replaced – or, to put it another way, because black life can be replaced, and it can be replaced because it is not singular – black people are thought not to die."

   Donna V. Jones, "Invidious Life"[54]

In a scene from the director's cut of Ari Aster's folk horror film *Midsommar* (2019), Josh (William Jackson Harper), a black anthropology student finishing his dissertation on European midsummer celebrations, reads a book called *The Secret Nazi Language of the Uthark*, the cover of which features a swastika and letters from the Scandinavian rune alphabet. This scene is perhaps the most obvious reference that Aster intends for the viewer to associate the Hårga with Nazism, which itself idealizes the Nordic "race." However, even in the official theatrical release of the film, from which the scene with the book is excluded, the disturbing signs of the white supremacist underpinnings of the commune are amply illustrated. That all the members of the cult are white Scandinavians makes logical sense considering the commune's closed-off placement in rural Sweden. That everyone is dressed in ethereal white and that the film is shot in a "whiteness" that "envelops the screen," to cite Noor Al-Sibai's review, is consonant with the perpetual daylight of a Scandinavian summer (Al-Sibai 2019). However, when we learn that members of the commune invite outsiders with whom to mate and – biologically, not racially – diversify the genetic pool, the concerted whiteness of the commune becomes evident. *Midsommar* emerges as a critique of the horrors of white supremacy, as well as a satire of environmental sustainability.

---

[53] Karera 2019: 34.   [54] Jones 2016: 234.

We confirm that the Hårga are a vitalist death cult thinly disguised as an eco-conscious commune when we witness the brutal *ättestupa* ceremony, during which two elders who have reached the age of seventy-two willingly jump to their deaths from a high cliff. Though one of them dies upon impact, the other survives and young Hårga girls are tasked with crushing his gruesomely injured head with giant mallets, a duty they perform with perfunctory seriousness. The cult's high priestess, Siv (Gunnel Fred), approaches the guests, who react to the ceremony with an understandable mixture of horror and surprise, and explains: "We view life as a circle, a recycle. The lady who jumped, her name was Ylva, yes? And that baby over there who is not yet born will inherit that name." Remaining alive beyond the age of seventy-two creates an unsustainable strain on the commune's resources. Surviving members thus are all healthy, young, and white, physically helpful to the running of the commune, in an echo of vitalist Nazi ideology. The sole exception to this eugenic principle is Ruben, who is "disabled" and plays the role of the cult's oracle.

The other sign that this is a white supremacist cult is how the non-white visitors fare. Unlike the white members of the commune and most of the white visitors, the black and other non-white visitors, without exception, die unceremoniously. Following the tradition of entitled, curious anthropologists (though, in this case, the anthropologist is black and the research subjects are white – and not in a mere inversion of power, for the black anthropologist will remain the mutilatable and desecrated despite his studies), Josh sneaks out at night to photograph the cult's sacred text and is bludgeoned to death. Christian, the white male protagonist, later sees a dark-skinned foot sticking out from the ground in a flower bed. In this scene, a naked Christian is fleeing a ritual in which he has ceremoniously mated with one of the Hårga women. His reproductive, white penis mirrors and inverts the phallic symbol of the black man's foot, which has no reproductive value to this cult but, instead, has the value of *being* compost. It is unclear whether the foot remains attached to Josh's body, which would then be buried underground. Either way, the foot's sticking out from the ground rather than being rendered a more readily usable form of compost that would not take as long to be "useful" renders this macabre burial both one of composting and of desecrating the black body. If there is "ceremony" here, it is that of the long history of the improper burials of black(ened) people (Dayan 1998 and Yaeger 2000). Whether or not this is a punishment for Josh's own desecration of the Hårga's sacred book, one assumes that Josh would have been murdered whether or not he had been caught soiling the sacred book with his black proximity.

Panic growing, Christian runs into a barn, where he sees another horrific sight. This time he sees Simon, a light-skinned black British guest, hanging from the ceiling by his flayed back skin while his lungs incredulously move with life. Chickens feed from his body, nurtured by his pained vitality. Like the black characters in *Get Out*, Simon has been condemned to a living death useful for others' lives; in this case the living beings are the fowl that may or may not end up becoming the Hårga's food. According to the interpretations in *Ariel's Ecology*, the purpose and definition of his "parahumanity" is thus fulfilled. While other characters die in the film, it is striking that it is the deaths, or living deaths, of the two black characters that perform the function of providing life for others in a continual desecration of their own bodies. This exposes the other side of the mantra "I will become compost": "you – the black – will be desecrated; you *are the* desecratable." In an interview, Ari Aster confirms that Josh is "thrown away in a way that the other members of the main cast are not ... And that is because these people have no further *use* for him" (Ganz 2019, emphasis added). Like Simon, his "use" emerges only through his (living) death.

When one of the *ättestupa* sacrifices remains grotesquely alive after jumping, he moans in "ecstatic and intolerable" pain (Batailles 1989: 206). The Hårga women then begin imitating his cries and moans. They replicate this ritual later when Dani (Florence Pugh), the protagonist, sobs after learning that her boyfriend Christian had mated with a commune member. (It is noteworthy that Dani and the rest of the commune are high on magic mushrooms during these midsummer rituals.) Xine Yao calls the scene in which the Hårga women surround Dani "white sympathy" and argues that "the feelings of white womanhood are given center stage and eventual catharsis" (Yao 2019). Though Aster's film is ultimately critical of the obvious white supremacy of the Hårga, it remains unclear whether it is also critical of Dani's bloodthirst surrounding her awful boyfriend. Or, more relevant to this Element, why does Dani's flattened and bizarre affect at the end of the film show no trace of empathy in relation to the other murdered guests?

Part of the problem of centralizing empathy or sympathy (in this case, the distinction between the two terms is irrelevant) as the emotive vehicle of effecting change – rather than as a self-indulgent affect – is that it leaves little to no room for black(ened) affect, especially rage. Dayan, for instance, argues that "abolitionist fictions thrived on the costs of sentiment, though such charitable pathos was costly only to those who were not white" (Dayan 1998: 316n9). Jasmine Nichole Cobb's analysis of the abolitionist image of the supplicant and half-nude black men and women begging to be freed by the empathetic white can be contrasted with the terrifying vigor and kinesis of the running maroon or revolting black, at times depicted holding an axe or machete. This latter image of a black person taking his or her freedom, rather than begging for it, does not prompt the requisite empathy from the white reader or viewer. Cobb focuses on an "antislavery handbag" that belonged to Angelina Grimké and that she wore to her 1838 wedding to abolitionist Theodore Weld. The handbag depicted a "bereaved Black mother" who "holds her head and looks down at what appears to be a deceased infant" (Cobb 2015: 167). The other side of the handbag featured the more common imagery of the "Kneeling Slave" emblem. Cobb interprets Grimké's decision to wear this handbag as an act that "symboliz[ed] White women's virtue by wearing the Black woman's body" (Cobb 2015: 168). Central to this portrayal, like so many others meant to cull white empathy or sympathy for black people's "humanity," is black suffering. To be blunt, the black infant must die for the white bride to communicate empathy in a public performance of her new role as abolitionist's wife.

A more recent instance of the pitfalls of white empathy is observable around Dana Schutz's controversial painting *Open Casket* (2016), which depicts in "abstracted but still vaguely figurative form" the photograph of Emmett Till's mutilated and tortured body (Raiford 2020). His mother, Mamie Till, had decided to share with the black press the horrific photograph of her child's tortured visage as a form of what Leigh Raiford describes as the "witnessing and testifying" in which the mourners who attended the funeral participated (Raiford 2011, 88). *Open Casket* and two other paintings were chosen by 2017 Whitney Biennial curators Mia Locks and Christopher Y. Lew as representative of Schutz's oeuvre and, by implication, U.S. contemporary painting for that year (Tomkins 2017). Contrasted with Mamie Till's "marshalling of the force and fury of her son Emmett Till's murder" in a world perhaps less inundated with the visual imagery of black suffering, in the context of that Whitney Biennial, "audiences, Black audiences especially," Leigh Raiford writes, "have been inundated with a seemingly endless loop of images of Black death at the hands of law enforcement and vigilantes" (Raiford 2011: 18 and 2020). Mamie Till's rage at what rapacious white men "protecting" a white woman did to her child transformed what the image of the suffering black body was for.[55] Schutz's painting turned the image of the tortured dead child into one that could yield pathos, as it did for her, rather than the political rage Mamie Till wanted to incite. The painting's inclusion in the Biennial, Raiford continues, "returns us to and depends upon the visual presence of the Black body (and the images that cathect around it) without offering a critical reading of systemic racist violence" (Raiford 2020).

Schutz defended herself from the subsequent outrage over her controversial painting: "It's a real event, and it's violence. But it has to be tender, and also about how it's been for his mother. I don't know, I'm trying. I'm talking too

---

[55] The white woman, Carolyn Bryant Donham, who had accused the fourteen-year-old child of whistling and making "verbal and physical advances on her," revealed that she had lied and claims to not recall the events that led to Till's torture and murder (Weller 2017).

much about it" (Tomkins 2017). In a later interview, Schutz states that she was attempting to "register this monstrous act and this tragic loss" (Loos 2019). In articles about Schutz and the controversy, members of the art world establishment repeat the mantra that the negative reaction to the painting "was a learning experience" (Loos 2019). This, combined with Schutz's seemingly incredulous repetition that Till's horrific murder "really happened" induces the question: what is the function of white empathy (Tomkins 2017)? While one may attribute empathy to "good intentions," Hartman muses on "the precariousness of empathy" and considers "the effort to counteract the commonplace callousness to black suffering [which] requires that the white body be positioned in the place of the black body in order to make this this suffering visible and intelligible" (Hartfman 1997, 19). "In making," she continues, "the other's suffering one's own, this suffering is occluded by the other's obliteration" (Hartman 1997, 19). The nineteenth-century white abolitionist empathy that Hartman writes about "must supplant the black captive in order to give expression to black suffering, and, as a consequence, the dilemma – the denial of black sentience and the obscurity of suffering – is not attenuated but instantiated" (Hartman 1997, 19).

Empathy or "sympathy" is also afoot in an earlier Schutz painting, *Autopsy of Michael Jackson* (2005), which depicts the corpse of the genitally mutilated (i.e., lynched) megastar. Because Schutz created this painting while Jackson was still alive and would be for four more years, could one consider this painting a work of "speculative fabulation"? (The "prescient" painting went up in value when Jackson died [Vartanian 2009]). In an interview with Mei Chin for *Bomb* magazine, Schutz describes her reasoning behind her choice to paint Jackson and to do so in that way:

> In some ways he's the most self-made man there is, to the point of it becoming really scary. I was thinking of the painting as a photograph that hasn't been taken yet. I posited all these question [*sic*] around Michael Jackson's death: How does he die? How old is he? What shape is he in? What does he look like naked? He ended up looking like just a dead man. Which for me was very strange. *I ended up having sympathy for him.* There is an immortality about him in life. In the painting there is an autopsy incision alluding to his insides, which is intrusive and contradicts the constant reforming of his external features. In the painting he is very mortal. (Chin 2006, emphasis added)

The "prescience" that art critic Hrag Vartanian ascribes to the painting after Jackson's death in 2009 is indiscernible from the will toward black death and mutilation behind the speculative futurities I have been describing throughout this Element. Here, however, there is no sublimation. There is only the mutilated black body and the white woman's fantasy of the black megastar, who, to her, looks dead already anyway. Jackson and his modernity – "self-made man" –

had "scared" Schutz, and so she must kill him (*"Maman,* look, a Negro; I'm scared!" [Fanon 2008: 112]). Schutz's impulse to portray the destroyed black man, whose biological aliveness also evokes a kind of living death and immortality, recalls Donna V. Jones's estimation that individual black lives defy the laws of nature: "Black life is replaced by more black life over the generations. It never dies. It is only replaced in the next generation; and because it is replaced – or, to put it another way, because black life can be replaced, and it can be replaced because it is not singular – black people are thought not to die" (Jones 2016: 234). In a sense, Schutz's painting withholds from Jackson his singularity as a megastar and the kind of immortality of fame. She instead brings him "down" to where he really belongs: as a slab of open flesh on a dissection table, open to Schutz's and other viewers' penetrating gaze and to the flashing blades of scientific-medical instruments ("To be white is to colonize the afterlife" [Benjamin 2018: 42]). Thinking with Hartman, Cobb, and Raiford prompts the question: does black suffering and death perform the function of producing empathy itself, as a kind of cathartic, recharging sentiment whose purpose is simply to regenerate itself for itself – that is, for whiteness' ipseity (Hartman 1997, 19)?

The entanglements between self and other evident in the production of white empathy echo what Haraway, biologist Lynn Margulis, and her son Dorion Sagan call "symbiosis," "symbiogenesis," and "becoming-with," terms that become metaphorized through the term "miscegenation" (Haraway 1989: 378–379 and 2016b, 148). "When advocating for the theory of symbiogenesis," writes Zakiyyah Jackson, "it seems to have gone unnoticed that Margulis and Sagan also present their theory in highly racialized terms, even occasionally referring to symbiotic cells as 'miscegenated'" (Jackson 2020: 153). Recall that the Camilles are biologically "miscegenated" with monarch butterflies. After the extinction of monarch butterflies, what remains are the humans – with and without symbionts – who endure on this planet at a population number that is more acceptable to ecological writers, including those with symbionts such as the butterflies. In Haraway's fabulation, the biological miscegenation between human and monarch butterfly that produces a Camille begets both the expected physical sensory shifts and a more nebulous and subtly spiritual interspecies empathy. By the era of Camille 2 (2085–2185), the urgent work of caring for the threatened futurity of monarch butterflies, as well as other chosen species, is inextricable from the literal biological intermixture with them. That is, worthwhile change cannot be achieved without a literalizing of empathy, which is only possible if one inhabits not just the imagined place, but the flesh of the other.

Eco-criticism views the human-induced tinkering necessary to conjure more ecological becoming-with with both wide-eyed optimism and steely resolution. It seems that the speculative mode that eco-critics enjoy both producing and promoting conceals destruction with productivity and replaces the horror of the dystopic with the pleasures of the utopic. Consider, for instance, critical ocean studies scholar Elizabeth DeLoughrey's interpretive process in her essay "Kinship in the Abyss," which focuses on *The Deep*, a black-authored novella about "aqueous merfolk named the wajinru" (DeLoughrey 2022: 1). The text states:

> This volume on kinship as a critical idiom in oceanic studies helps suture this topic to the *vital* questions raised by Christina Sharpe's "wake work" alongside the generative relations imagined in Edouard Glissant's theory of the middle passage as a "womb abyss"; a descent into the abjection and terror of colonial anti-black violence as well as a generative space of alterity and becoming. To Glissant, Sharpe, and many other hydro-theorists, the Atlantic Ocean provides the ontological and material space for the history of modernity as well as a figure for the possibilities of regeneration. (DeLoughrey 2022, 1, emphasis added)

Sharpe's concept of wake work concerns itself with healing and mourning in the wake of terroristic and relentless anti-black violence. "What does it mean to defend the dead?" writes Sharpe. "To tend to the Black dead and dying: to tend to the Black person, to Black people, always living in the push toward our death? It means work: hard emotional, physical, and intellectual work that demands vigilant attendance to the needs of the dying, to ease their way, and also to the needs of the living" (Sharpe 2016, 10). Sharpe articulates a "we" here that is unquestionably about black people. It is unclear, then, how DeLoughrey's essay renders Sharpe's "we" "vital" for all. As with much of his oeuvre, Glissant's concept of the "womb abyss" remains somewhat ambivalent in that one wonders what his poesis of black Caribbean specificities in the Caribbean opened to *tout-monde*. To the point, the interpretive process in DeLoughrey's article gathers concepts that attend to the violence of the Middle Passage and the legacies of slavery in order to transform these and the material space of the violence itself as generative. One may initially understand this generativity to be one for the benefit of those bearing the brunt of this violence, namely the descendants of those who survived the Middle Passage, a rhetorical move that would also confound. The end of the essay, however, clarifies any potential confusion; as with other ecological writings, this generativity serves the interests of a planetary "we" that, as I have shown, is far from all-inclusive. "Thinking at multiple scales of nonhuman kinship," concludes DeLoughrey,

> – from waijinru [*sic*] to sharks to seawater to the bacteria of the womb abyss – *we* can submerge in a speculative way with the queer ocean ecologies of *The Deep*. In this way the womb abyss becomes a figure of generation and "super life" in ways that fundamentally challenge *our* own anthropocentric frameworks of kinship, expanding them to the yet-unimagined life of neural networks. The meaning *we* can attribute to being "born of the dead," as the authors query, is to be agents and

co-creators of the womb abyss, participants in a queer alterity of a more-than-human ontology of the ever changing sea. (DeLoughrey 2022: 9, emphasis added)

One can only guess what it means that "we" can be "co-creators" of the womb abyss, when the womb abyss as a concept is inseparable both from the historical event and aftermath of the Middle Passage *and* the sexual and reproductive violence black women historically bore and the wake of the association between black women and sexual availability. This textual example gives evidence to the danger in "scraping" the historical "barnacles" off signifiers and concepts, such as the womb abyss, as poetic as some may find them to be. *The Deep* may indeed generalize a history of violence suffered by a specific part of the global population, a generalization that DeLoughrey's article accepts as is. Or the procedures in this article may exemplify, as many other ecological writings also exemplify, how the non-black ecological writer tucks herself into a particular history of suffering, not as a descendent and beneficiary of the perpetrators of the violence, but in a generalized "we" facilitated by the speculative mode.

The speculative has a long history in black writing and creativity due to its function as a rhetorical escape valve from relentless anti-black violence. Methods of speculation or fabulation have also been useful for scholars who must contend with archival gaps when attempting to reconstruct historical black social and cultural life. What I critique here is the marshalling of the speculative to rush over historical, rhetorical, and philosophical accountings of unending anti-black forms of genocidal violence. The close readings I conducted throughout this Element bely the insistence that "we" "already know" the extent and depth of the violence. If "we" "already know," then why does black suffering continue to facilitate generativity for an exclusive "all"? If "we" "already know," then why is negative critique that withholds a relief already withheld by the world – for some – faced with such forceful dismissal and silencing in current US academic spaces?

While speculative narratives tend to harbor utopian fantasies of the past, present, and future, horror narratives show precisely "for whom both the Anthropocene and its apocalyptic imaginaries do not necessarily hold any emancipating value" (Karera 2019: 34). What I have sought to show throughout *This Will Not Be Generative* is that this horror lurks beneath the ludic and "generative" language of ecological writings. They cannot metaphorize their way out of genocidal logics.

What might it mean to cultivate an ethics that does not rely on a "deathly intimacy," a collapse with the other, which requires the other's destruction for the subject's becoming-with (Haraway citing Philip J. Hilts in Haraway and Nichols Goodeve 2000: 75)? I do not to have a complete answer to this difficult question. I want to honor the title of this Element, but I will gesture toward some closing remarks.

That climate change discourses "undermine" subject-centered humanist thought does not concern me; rather, the concern is that the writings I have explored in this Element cannot seem to imagine what comes after the (white) human, whether we call the human a "subject," a "Camille," or a "rooted white *indigène*." This writing remains staunchly anthropocentric even as it slyly seeks to slip out of the category. How else to understand the grammar of being in Wells's "to be a field of poppies" or of Haraway's symbiosis that always includes some facet of non-black human agency? Speculative fabulation costumes narratives of whiteness's survival in the garb of an obviously exclusionary "we," as well as in the language of "care," "love," "curiosity," and "politeness."

To be radically anti-humanist may look like a future that entirely excludes us – here, the "we" is all homo sapiens – a future that eco-critics never seem capable of imagining – perhaps because it's not a question of imagining, but reading, given that for some of us, and the generations that bore us, the destruction they claim to fear is simply our history. Perhaps to be in a black(ened) position is to always face a vision of the world that violently seeks to exterminate our specific "we." Perhaps this is too nihilistic a perspective and they will just say that there is no room for nihilism in this vision of the world's end. Just endless possibility, for some. "We" always includes "me" and generatively excludes "them."

References

Al-Sibai, N. (2019). In "Midsommar," Silent White Supremacy Shrieks Volumes. www.truthdig.com/articles/in-midsommar-silent-white-supremacy-shrieks-volumes.

Allewaert, M. (2013). *Ariel's Ecology*. University of Minnesota Press.

Amuse-Bouche. *Hannibal* (2013). April 11.

Aravamudan, S. (2013). The Catachronism of Climate Change. *diacritics*, 41(3), 6–30.

Bataille, G. (1989). *The Tears of Eros*. Translated by P. Connor. City Lights Books.

Beauvoir-Dominique, R. (1995). Underground Realms of Being: Vodoun Magic. In D. J. Consentino, ed., *Sacred Arts of Haitian Vodou*. UCLA Fowler Museum of Cultural History, pp. 153–179.

Benjamin, R. (2018). Black AfterLives Matter: Cultivating Kinfulness As Reproductive Justice. In *Making Kin Not Population: Reconceiving Generations*. Prickly Paradigm Press, pp. 41–65.

Best, S. and Marcus, S. (2009). Surface Reading: An Introduction. *Representations*, 108(1), 1–21.

Carroll, L. (2012). *Jabberwocky and Other Nonsense*. Penguin UK.

Césaire, A. (2000). *Discourse on Colonialism*. Translated by J. Pinkham. Monthly Review Press.

Chin, M. (2006). *Dana Schutz*. www.bombmagazine.org/articles/dana-schutz.

Chow, R. (1998). *Ethics after Idealism: Theory-Culture-Ethnicity-Reading*. Indiana University Press.

Chow, R. (2021). *A Face Drawn in Sand: Humanistic Inquiry and Foucault in the Present*. Columbia University Press.

Clarke, A. E. and Haraway, D. J. (2018). *Making Kin Not Population*. Prickly Paradigm Press.

Clifford, J. (1999). *Routes: Travel and Translation in the Late Twentieth Century*. Harvard University Press.

Cobb, J. N. (2015). *Picture Freedom: Remaking Black Visuality in the Early Nineteenth Century*. New York University Press.

Colebrook, C. (2016). What Is the Anthropo-political? In *Twilight of the Anthropocene Idols*. Open Access, pp. 81–125. www.library.oapen.org/handle/20.500.12657/32930.

Cooper, C. M. (2022). Fallen: Generation, Postlapsarian Verticality + the Black Chthonic. *Rhizomes: Cultural Studies in Emerging Knowledge*, 38.

Davis, J., Moulton, A. A., Van Sant, L., and Williams, B. (2019). Anthropocene, Capitalocene, . . . Plantationocene? A Manifesto for Ecological Justice in an Age of Global Crises. *Geography Compass*, 13(5).

Dayan, C. [J.] (1998). *Haiti, History, and The Gods*. University of California Press.

Dayan, C. (2015). *With Dogs at the Edge of Life*. Columbia University Press.

Dayan, C. (2020). *Animal Quintet: A Southern Memoir*. Los Angeles Review of Books.

Deloria, P. J. (1998). *Playing Indian*. Yale University Press.

DeLoughrey, E. (2022). Kinship in the Abyss: Submerging with *The Deep*. *Atlantic Studies*. Published online June 27.

Derrida, J. (2008). *The Animal That Therefore I Am*. Translated by D. Wills. Fordham University Press.

Ellis Neyra, R. (2020). The Question of Ethics in the Semiotics of Brownness. *sx salon*, 35. www.smallaxe.net/sxsalon/discussions/question-ethics-semiotics-brownness.

Fanon, F. (2008). *Black Skin, White Masks*. Grove Press.

Ferreira da Silva, D. (2014). Toward a Black Feminist Poethics. *The Black Scholar*, 44(2), 81–97.

Forbes, J. D. (2010). Black Pioneers: The Spanish-Speaking Afro-Americans of the Southwest. In *The Afro-Latin@ Reader: History and Culture in the United States*. Duke University Press, pp. 27–37.

Galli, J. (n.d.). *The Life of Fin* (2018). www.youtube.com/watch?v=7Vv9V-K7wc0.

Ganz, J. (2019). *Ari Aster and "Midsommar" Cast Sound Off On Hypnotic Horror's Most Chilling Scenes*. www.nydailynews.com/entertainment/movies/ny-midsommar-spoilers-director-cast-20190707-maozoxfru5btjinq7ax6nerorq-story.html.

Get Out. (2017). Universal Pictures.

Goldberg, M. (2017). *Get Out*: Darker Alternate Ending Revealed by Jordan Peele. www.collider.com/get-out-alternate-ending.

Greenberg, A. (2000). *A Chemical History Tour: Picturing Chemistry from Alchemy to Modern Molecular Science*. John Wiley & Sons.

Haraway, D. J. (1981). In the Beginning Was the Word: The Genesis of Biological Theory. *Signs: Journal of Women in Culture and Society*, 6(3), 469–481.

Haraway, D. J. (1989). *Primate Visions: Gender, Race, and Nature in the World of Modern Science*. Routledge.

Haraway, D. J. (1991). The Promises of Monsters: A Regenerative Politics for Inappropriate/d Others. In *Cultural Studies*. Routledge, pp. 295–336.

Haraway, D. J. (2008). *When Species Meet*. University of Minnesota Press.

Haraway, D. J. (2016a). A Cyborg Manifesto: Science, Technology, and Socialist-Feminism in the Late Twentieth Century. In *Manifestly Haraway*. University of Minnesota Press, pp. 5–90.

Haraway, D. J. (2016b). *Staying with the Trouble: Making Kin in the Chthulucene*. Duke University Press.

Haraway, D. J., Ishikawa, N., Gilbert, S. F., et al. (2015). Anthropologists Are Talking – About the Anthropocene. *Ethnos*, 81(3), 535–564.

Haraway, D. J. and Nichols Goodeve, T. (2000). *How Like a Leaf: An Interview with Thyrza Nichols Goodeve*. Routledge.

Hartman, S. V. (1997). *Scenes of Subjection: Terror, Slavery, and Self-Making in Nineteenth-Century America*. Oxford University Press.

Hauck, D. W. (2008). *The Complete Idiot's Guide to Alchemy*. Alpha.

Hendrikx, B. (n.d.). *Are You Waste or Compost?* www.loop-of-life.com.

Henley, J. (2020). *First Funeral Held Using "Living Coffin" Made of Mushroom Fibre*. www.theguardian.com/society/2020/sep/15/first-funeral-living-coffin-made-mushroom-fibre-netherlands.

Holiday, H. (2019). *The First Angel of the Future: Sun Ra's Heliocentric Poetics for after the End of the World by Harmony Holiday*. www.poetryfoundation.org/harriet-books/2019/10/the-first-angel-of-the-future-sun-ras-heliocentric-poetics-for-after-the-end-of-the-world.

Hoofd, I. M. (2017). Book Review: Staying with the Trouble: Making Kin in the Chthulucene. *Feminist Review*, 117, 208–209.

Jackson, Z. I. (2020). *Becoming Human: Matter and Meaning in an Antiblack World*. New York University Press.

Johnson, S. E. (2012). *The Fear of French Negroes*: Transcolonial Collaboration in the Revolutionary Americas. University of California Press.

Johnson, S. E. (2018). "Your Mother Gave Birth to a Pig": Power, Abuse, and Planter Linguistics in Baudry des Lozière's *Vocabulaire Congo*. *Early American Studies*, 16(1), 7–40.

Jones, D. V. (2010) *The Racial Discourses of Life Philosophy: Négritude, Vitalism, and Modernity*. Columbia University Press.

Jones, D. V. (2016). Invidious Life. In *Against Life*. Northwestern University Press, pp. 231–256.

Jung, C. G. and Schwartz-Salant, N. (1995). *Jung on Alchemy*. Princeton University Press.

Karera, A. (2019). Blackness and the Pitfalls of Anthropocene Ethics. *Critical Philosophy of Race*, 7(1), 32–56.

Kincaid, J. (2000). *A Small Place*. Farrar, Straus and Giroux.

Loos, T. (2019). *After the Quake, Dana Schutz Gets Back to Work*. www
.nytimes.com/2019/01/09/arts/design/dana-schutz-painting-emmett-till-petzel-
gallery.html.

Marriott, D. (2000). *On Black Men*. Columbia University Press.

Mbembe, A. (2001). *On the Postcolony*. University of California Press.

Midsommar. (2019). A24.

Mitman, G. (2019). A Conversation with Donna Haraway and Anna Tsing.
www.edgeeffects.net/haraway-tsing-plantationocene.

Morrison, T. (1992). *Playing in the Dark: Whiteness and the Literary
Imagination*. Vintage Books.

Palmer, T. S. (2020). Otherwise Than Blackness. *Qui Parle*, 29(2), 247–283.

Paulson, S. (2019). Making Kin: An Interview with Donna Haraway. www
.lareviewofbooks.org/article/making-kin-an-interview-with-donna-haraway.

Pratt, M. L. (2007). *Imperial Eyes: Travel Writing and Transculturation*. 2nd ed.
Routledge.

Raiford, L. (2011). *Imprisoned in a Luminous Glare: Photography and the
African American Freedom Struggle*. University of North Carolina Press.

Raiford, L. (2020). Burning All Illusion: Abstraction, Black Life, and the
Unmaking of White Supremacy. *Art Journal*, 79(4), 76–91.

Ramírez-D'Oleo, D. (2018). *Colonial Phantoms: Belonging and Refusal in the
Dominican Americas, from the 19th Century to the Present*. New York
University Press.

Ramírez-D'Oleo, D. (2019a). *The Hills Are Alive: "Pet Sematary" and the
Horror of Indigenous Sovereignty and Black Freedom*. www.lareviewofbooks
.org/article/the-hills-are-alive-pet-sematary-and-the-horror-of-indigenous-
sovereignty-and-black-freedom.

Ramírez-D'Oleo, D. (2019b). Mushrooms and Mischief: On Questions of
Blackness. *Small Axe*, 23 (2), 152–163.

Ramírez-D'Oleo, D. (2021a). *Introduction to Caribbean, Gardener. ASAP/J*.
www.asapjournal.com/caribbean-gardener-introduction-dixa-ramirez-doleo.

Ramírez-D'Oleo, D. (2021b). Marronage, De Profundis. *Seen by Blackstar*.
www.blackstarfest.org/seen/read/issue-002/marronage-de-profundis.

Ramírez-D'Oleo, D. (2022). Insolence, Indolence, and the Ayitian Free Black.
Interventions, 24(7), 1011–1028.

Ravindranathan, T. (2018). "This Thick and Fibrous Now": A Review of Donna
Haraway's Manifestly Haraway and Staying with the Trouble: Making Kin in
the Chthulucene. *Postmodern Culture*, 28(2).

Schuller, K. (2018). *The Biopolitics of Feeling: Race, Sex, and Science in the
Nineteenth Century*. Duke University Press.

Schwartz-Salant, N. (1995). Introduction. In *Jung on Alchemy*. Princeton University Press, pp. 1–43.

Sedgwick, E.K. (2003). Paranoid Reading and Reparative Reading, Or, You Probably Think This Essay Is about You. In *Touching Feeling: Affect, Pedagogy, Performativity*. Duke University Press, pp. 123–151.

Sexton, J. (2016). Afro-pessimism: The Unclear Word. *Rhizomes: Cultural Studies in Emerging Knowledge*, 29.

Sharpe, C. E. (2016). *In the Wake: On Blackness and Being*. Duke University Press.

Sontag, S. (2002). Fascinating Fascism. In *Under the Sign of Saturn*. Farrar, Straus and Giroux, pp. 73–108.

Spivak, G. C. (1999). *A Critique of Postcolonial Reason: Toward a History of the Vanishing Present*. Harvard University Press.

Stengers, I. and Despret, V. (2014). *Women Who Make a Fuss: The Unfaithful Daughters of Virginia Woolf*. Translated by A. Knutson. University Of Minnesota Press.

Strathern, M., Sasser, J. S., Clarke, A. et al. (2019). Forum on Making Kin Not Population: Reconceiving Generations. *Feminist Studies*, 45(1), 159–172.

Stuelke, P. (2021). *The Ruse of Repair*. Duke University Press.

Terada, R. (2019). Hegel's Racism for Radicals. *Radical Philosophy*, 2.05, 11–22.

Terrefe, S. (2020). The Pornotrope of Decolonial Feminism. *Critical Philosophy of Race*, 8(1–2), 134–164.

Thompson, K. A. (2006). *An Eye for the Tropics: Tourism, Photography, and Framing the Caribbean Picturesque*. Duke University Press.

Tomkins, C. (2017). Why Dana Schutz Painted Emmett Till. The *New Yorker*. 3 April. www.newyorker.com/magazine/2017/04/10/why-dana-schutz-painted-emmett-till.

Vartanian, H. (2009). *Dana Schutz' Prescient "Autopsy of Michael Jackson" (2005)*. www.hragvartanian.com/2009/06/27/dana-schutz-mj.

Vicuña, C. (2019). *Cecilia Vicuña on M. NourbeSe Philip's "Zong!"* www.frieze.com/article/cecilia-vicuna-m-nourbese-philips-zong.

Vicuña, C. (n.d.). *Biography*. www.ceciliavicuna.com/biography.

Warren, C. L. (2018). *Ontological Terror: Blackness, Nihilism, and Emancipation*. Duke University Press.

Weigel, M. (2019). A Giant Bumptious Litter: Donna Haraway on Truth, Technology, and Resisting Extinction. *Logic*. www.logicmag.io/nature/a-giant-bumptious-litter.

Weller, S. (2017). How Author Timothy Tyson Found the Woman at the Center of the Emmett Till Case. *Vanity Fair*. www.vanityfair.com/news/2017/01/

how-author-timothy-tyson-found-the-woman-at-the-center-of-the-emmett-till-case?mbid=social_twitter.

Wells, L. (2021a). *Believers*. Farrar, Straus and Giroux.

Wells, L. (2021b). To Be a Field of Poppies. *Harper's Magazine*, October, pp. 36–44.

Wexler, L. (2000). *Tender Violence: Domestic Visions in an Age of U.S. Imperialism*. University of North Carolina Press.

Wilderson, F. B. (2010). *Red, White & Black: Cinema and the Structure of U.S. Antagonisms*. Duke University Press.

Williams, E. (1944). *Capitalism and Slavery*. University of North Carolina Press.

Yaeger, P. (2000). *Dirt and Desire: Reconstructing Southern Women's Writing, 1930–1990*. University of Chicago Press.

Yao, X. (2019). *Midsommar: The Horrors of White Sympathy*. https://avidly.lareviewofbooks.org/2019/08/13/midsommar-the-horrors-of-white-sympathy.

Acknowledgments

I would like to thank Marina Bilbija, Anne Eller, Greta LaFleur, and Ren Ellis Neyra for reading drafts of this Element. Special gratitude goes to Ren for their patient listening during the months of reading and writing that led to this volume, as well as to Benjamin Brewer, Axelle Karera, and Ronald Mendoza-de Jesús, who humored numerous discussions of my analyses and provided suggestions. Thanks also to Joanna Radin and the two anonymous reviewers, whose insights from within the fields of History of Science and STS were helpful to framing some of my arguments. I appreciated the comments and questions I received from my Brown University colleagues and students, who heard a very early version of what would become this Element in a talk I gave for the English Department in 2021 and from the participants and audience members of the History of Science Workshop 2023 at Princeton University, organized by Erika L. Milam and Banu Subramaniam, who read a short excerpt of a later draft. A hearty thanks to the series editors, especially Juno Jill Richards, for the invitation to write an Element and for their openness to the topic. Finally, thanks to the students in my 2019 graduate seminar "The Homo Sapiens at the End of the World," who helped me detect the violent undercurrents in some ecological writings.

I was pregnant with my daughter while writing this volume, reminding me both of my ambivalence towards narratives of futurity and my desire for her to know when and how to practice refusal. I dedicate this book to her.

Cambridge Elements ≡

Feminism and Contemporary Critical Theory

Jennifer Cooke
Loughborough University

Jennifer Cooke is Reader in Contemporary Literature and Theory at Loughborough University. She's author of *Contemporary Feminist Life-Writing: The New Audacity* (2020) and editor of *The New Feminist Literary Studies* (2020), *Scenes of Intimacy: Reading, Writing and Theorizing Contemporary Literature* (2013), and a special issue of *Textual Practice* on challenging intimacies and psychoanalysis (September 2013). Her first monograph is *Legacies of Plague in Literature, Theory and Film* (2009). Her research interests lie in theories of intimacy, the affective turn and theories of the emotions, queer and feminist theories, and contemporary literature. She chaired the Gendered Lives Research Group from 2015 to 2020.

Amber Jamilla Musser
CUNY Graduate Center

Amber Jamilla Musser is Professor of English at the CUNY Graduate Center. She is the author of *Sensational Flesh: Race, Power, and Masochism* (2014), *Sensual Excess: Queer Femininity and Brown Jouissance* (2018), and co-editor with Kadji Amin and Roy Peréz of a special issue of *ASAP Journal* on Queer Form (May 2017). She has also published extensively, including essays in *Feminist Theory, differences, Social Text, GLQ, and Women and Performance* on the intersections of critical race theory, sexuality studies, queer of color critique, black feminisms, and aesthetics.

Juno Jill Richards
Yale University

Juno Jill Richards is Associate Professor in English and affiliated faculty in Women, Gender, & Sexuality Studies at Yale University. They are the author of *The Fury Archives: Female Citizenship, Human Rights, and the International Avant-Gardes* (2020) and a co-author of *The Ferrante Letters: An Experiment in Collective Criticism* (2020). Their research focuses on queer/trans archives, social reproduction, critical legal theory, queer feminist science studies, disability justice, and 20th/21st century literature.

About the Series

Elements in Feminism and Contemporary Critical Theory provides a forum for interdisciplinary feminist scholarship that speaks directly to the contemporary moment. Grounded in queer, trans, antiracist, and intersectional feminist traditions, the series expands familiar paradigms of academic writing, locating new methods and modes to account for transformational feminist politics today.

Cambridge Elements ≡

Feminism and Contemporary Critical Theory

Elements in the Series

This Will Not Be Generative
Dixa Ramírez-D'Oleo

A full series listing is available at: www.cambridge.org/EFCT

Printed in the United States
by Baker & Taylor Publisher Services